DATE DUE

Creating

Active

Learning

Creating Active Learning

with examples drawn
from the social sciences

Larry Litecky

COMMUNITY COLLEGE PRESS®

a division of the American Association of
Community Colleges

Washington, D.C.

Credits

The author gratefully acknowledges the following individuals and publishers for permission to include excerpts from their works. Full citations are included in the bibliography on pages 75 and 76.

xiii: Excerpt from *An American Imperative: Higher Expectations for Higher Education* (Wingspread Group on Higher Education 1993) reprinted by permission of The Johnson Foundation, Inc., Racine, Wis.

2: Excerpt from *Taxonomy of Educational Objectives,* by Benjamin S. Bloom, © 1956 by Longman. Reprinted by permission of Addison Wesley Educational Publishers, Inc.

2: Table 1.1 reproduced from *Critical Thinking: Educational Imperative* (Barnes 1992) by permission of Jossey-Bass, San Francisco.

3: Table 1.2 reproduced from *Teaching Thinking: Issues and Approaches* (Schwartz and Perkins 1990) by permission of Critical Thinking Books & Software, P.O. Box 448, Pacific Grove, Calif., 93950, (800) 458-4849.

3: Excerpt from *Critical Thinking: Educational Imperative* (Barnes 1992) reprinted by permission of Jossey-Bass, San Francisco.

3–4: Thinking F.I.R.E. model reproduced by permission of Joel Peterson.

5: Excerpt from *Promoting Active Learning* (Meyers and Jones 1993) reprinted by permission of Jossey-Bass, San Francisco.

7: Table 1.4, "Critical Thinking and the Multiple Dimensions of Learning," reproduced by permission of Simon & Schuster, from *The Paideia Proposal* by Mortimer J. Adler, © 1982 by the Institute for Philosophical Research.

10: Excerpt from "Seven Principles for Good Practice in Undergraduate Education" (Chickering and Gamson 1990) reprinted by permission of The Johnson Foundation, Inc., Racine, Wis.

11: Excerpt from *Critical Thinking and Education* (McPeck 1981), © John McPeck, reprinted by permission of St. Martin's Press, Inc.

22: Figure 3.2 reproduced from *Critical Thinking: Educational Imperative* (Barnes 1992) by permission of Jossey-Bass, San Francisco.

44: Excerpt from *Collaborative Learning: A Sourcebook for Higher Education* (Goodsell, et al. 1992) reprinted by permission of the National Center on Postsecondary Teaching, Learning, & Assessment, Pennsylvania State University, University Park, Pa.

Requests for permission should be sent to
Community College Press
American Association of Community Colleges
One Dupont Circle, NW
Suite 410
Washington, DC 20036
(202) 728-0200

Printed in the United States of America.

ISBN 0-87117-310-7

Contents

Preface

This book arises from my experience of more than two decades as a college classroom teacher. Although I have taught in Australia and Arizona, most of my experience has been in Minnesota, at the state universities, independent colleges, and, primarily, at Minneapolis Community College.

In teaching more than 35 different courses in a variety of disciplines, ranging from humanities and philosophy to political science and sociology, I became aware of a common thread about my goals in teaching. Each course had two goals for students:

- acquisition of a body of information and interpretation
- development of thinking skills, both critical and creative

When I began teaching, my attention was overwhelmingly focused on the first goal—the subject matter. I drew on the models of good teachers I had known. I tried to organize my lectures well and to gain a command of the information so that my lecture notes would be superfluous. I used a repertoire of stories and anecdotes to create a bond with students. In short, I set out to become the best lecturer I could. Although eventually I tried to move beyond lecturing, I believe it is a necessary step in becoming a good teacher.

In the early 1980s, I began to teach three- to four-hour classes and concluded that only a fool would lecture for this time. I began to structure courses with time blocks for student activity.

As I began to design activities for students, I saw the activities as a way for students to achieve the second course goal—the development of thinking skills, both critical and creative. Each discipline and each course has models of thinking and criteria for what thinking well means. I came to believe that for students to develop their ability to think well, they need practice in thinking. The activities were the opportunities for student practice.

Developing intellectual skills may be considered analogous to developing motor skills. A tennis instructor would never expect a student to develop as a tennis player by merely watching and listening to the instructor. The student needs to play. In a college education, a student needs an opportunity to think—and to receive feedback on that thinking—in order to develop as a thinker.

I came to believe that the goal of student learning, and of teaching to develop that learning, was not well served by a primary reliance on lecturing. Lecturing tends to foster passivity on the part of students and to limit intellectual activity to memorization and recall. For students to learn, they need to become active in the educational process. They need to become doers. I now ask myself repeatedly,

What will students do to achieve the goals of this course, of this discipline?

By engaging in the response to this question, my focus has been to create active learning strategies in the context of traditional classroom-based courses. These classroom strategies are designed so that students engage in learning activities—nearly always in writing and speaking. Sometimes they write and speak about something that they have listened to or read; sometimes they write and speak about something they have done, as through service learning or field experience. The key idea is to do something to engage students in their thinking about the subject matter of the course.

I have come to believe that the design of these active learning strategies entails artistry and craftsmanship. It is possible to design these strategies so poorly that they are a total waste of time. It is also possible to design them with purpose, detail, and structure so that they give birth to real student learning, thinking, and understanding.

It is my goal in this book to further the practice of good teaching and the teaching of thinking. I believe that the time is ripe for faculty to share with each other how to teach, by focusing on what they ask their students to do.

Over the past dozen years, I have attended some 70 conferences dealing with different aspects of teaching and learning. In this time, four major movements have evolved to improve college teaching and learning:

◆ critical thinking

◆ writing across the curriculum

◆ collaborative, cooperative learning

◆ classroom assessment

I have observed a great willingness among the research universities, comprehensive universities, and independent four-year colleges to theorize about these movements. However, few practitioners from these sectors share what they actually do in their courses.

On the other hand, the community colleges display a willingness to enter the arena of the practitioner. At concurrent sessions at conferences, in their own colleges and systems, community college faculty are entering into conversations about how to engage students in active learning strategies. This book is built on those conversations about what works and what does not.

In my own development as a college teacher, I have found the sharing of specific information with another faculty member to be most helpful. When someone shows me an assignment or describes an in-class activity, I can incorporate that information into my own teaching. My hope is that the written active learning strategies in this book will assist other higher education faculty in developing student thinking and content mastery. Ideally, each discipline and each course will build a menu of active learning strategies. Faculty can then select and amend this menu to strengthen their own teaching.

An ideal place to begin this process is in the community college, in part because the teaching mission of community colleges, and of their faculties, is unencumbered by the research mission. In addition, the practical expertise on "how to teach" resides in a greater concentration on community college campuses than elsewhere. By drawing on the expertise within community colleges, I hope that the knowledge of how to teach and how to use active learning strategies will spread to other sectors of American higher education.

SUMMARY

The introduction sets the learning and teaching context for the chapters and conclusion. It establishes the importance of a positive classroom climate and of engaging student interest at the beginning of a course. The six chapters examine the intricate web of active learning strategies and thinking to achieve learning. They are united in their focus on making the student an active thinker through specific writing and speaking activities.

Chapter 1, "Fostering Critical Thinking through Writing and Speaking Strategies," is a theoretical beginning. It examines the importance of teaching students to think well and looks at some definitions of what that process entails. The chapter concludes by calling for the need to articulate to students how they can develop as thinkers.

Chapter 2, "Critical Thinking in the Social Sciences," moves from generic definitions to a discipline-based definition of the critical thinking abilities and skills in the social sciences. The chapter contains a detailed examination of these habits of the mind.

Chapter 3, "Writing in the Disciplines: Fostering Critical Thinking," the longest chapter in the book, contains 86 activities for students. They range from in-class, nongraded "short writes" to assignments and tests. Any of these writing activi-

ties can also be linked to discussion—either in small groups or with the entire class.

Chapter 4, "Spoken Thought: Collaborative, Cooperative Learning and Socratic Exchanges," examines the values of conversation and the spoken word in making students better thinkers. Thirty-two examples of how to use speaking in active learning strategies constitute this chapter.

Chapter 5, "The Critical Thinking Process: Writing and Speaking to Make Thinking Explicit across the Curriculum," moves to specific learning activities. This chapter has 30 activities designed to make students aware of the thinking process in general and of the key structured thought processes in the discipline in particular.

Chapter 6, "Classroom Assessment: Thinking about Thinking, Teaching, and Learning," points out the importance of assessment and feedback for both students and teachers. Twenty-four examples of written assessment are listed.

The conclusion comments on the need to expand these examples in a conversation to deepen the culture of teaching and learning. Sharing teaching and learning strategies will improve faculty members as teacher-learners and students as learner-thinkers.

Acknowledgments

I would like to thank my wife and life partner, Donna, for her support of my faculty activities throughout the past 26 years. In addition, my children, Rachel and Sara, have provided me with great support over the years.

My colleagues in faculty development within Minnesota's community colleges deserve special recognition. Walter Cullen, Norma Rowe, Connie Mierendorf, Joel Peterson, and Connie Stack are prominent among those colleagues.

I received great support for my pursuits in faculty development from the members of the Minnesota Community College Faculty Association (MCCFA). As the elected president of that organization, I owe much to the faculty around Minnesota who supported me so enthusiastically. In particular, I want to thank MCCFA's staff, Michele Van Gemert and Marge Stewart, for their invaluable assistance in preparing the manuscript.

Introduction

In *An American Imperative* (1993), the Wingspread Group on Higher Education, a group of 16 individuals brought together by the Johnson Foundation, Inc., to draft an open letter to those concerned with the American future, asserts that a mismatch exists between what American society needs from higher education and what it is receiving. To rectify that mismatch, the Wingspread Group believes that higher education must

◆ model the values that matter to the colleges, universities, and society, and develop a required liberal education curriculum;

◆ make the student-learner the highest priority and improve teaching practices to help students attain higher levels of educational achievement; and

◆ foster collaboration between higher education and all other institutions involved in learning.

This book addresses the second item, improving teaching and learning, by focusing on both the means and the ends of teaching and learning. If faculty members improve teaching and learning, then the teaching and learning of values also can improve, and higher education will have an enhanced ability to share with other learning institutions.

In 1991, the U.S. Department of Labor issued the Secretary's Commission on Achieving Necessary Skills (SCANS) reports on work preparedness. The reports recognize that passivity may have been adequate for work on the assembly line in the past but is inadequate today. High-performance work requires workers with a solid foundation in the basic literacy and computational skills; in the thinking skills necessary to put knowledge to work; and in the personal qualities of dedicated, trustworthy workers. In addition to this foundation, effective workers need to be able to use and understand resources, systems, technology, information, and interpersonal skills.

While these work goals are laudable, achieving them in the present social and cultural context is a real challenge. A person may hold several jobs and more than one career in a lifetime. Flexibility and similar critical dispositions will be required for effective learning, living, and working.

CHALLENGES FACING COLLEGE STUDENTS

The traditional pre–World War II college student was young, full time, intellectually prepared, single, nonworking, and residential. More likely than not, the student was also upper middle class, white, and male.

In the post–World War II evolution of the community colleges, none of these characteristics survive as dominant. Today 66 percent of community college students work and 63 percent attend on a part-time basis. Fifty-eight percent are women, and 29.5 percent of community college students are members of minority groups. Eight percent report a disability. The age range of students has become more varied, with an average student age of 29 years (*National Profile* 1997). Many students have family responsibilities. Compared with other higher education students, a disproportionate number of community college students are from economically disadvantaged and culturally diverse backgrounds. Many need remedial assistance in reading, writing, and mathematics in order to be successful in their continued studies.

The classroom profile is varied. For example, in some urban community colleges a group of 35 students might include three African American men over the age of 25, three students in wheelchairs, six Southeast Asian adults, four white men over the age of 30 who are retraining for new jobs, six white women reentering education after raising their families, 10 recent high school graduates, and three Native Americans who dropped out of high school 20 years ago. The majority of these people work, have family responsibilities, share some fear about school, and need some brushup on their skills.

College students represent different social and cultural backgrounds and bring with them a broad range of academic preparation. Many community college assessment tests reveal that more than 50 percent of entering students need better academic preparation to do college-level work.

The pressures on society as a whole manifest themselves in community college students. The commuter nature of community colleges, combined with part-time enrollment patterns, results in anonymity among students. Work and family responsibilities fragment the time of many students, so they cannot devote time to activities and assignments beyond the classroom. Many features of modern life—including television—promote boredom, passivity, and disengagement. Students reared in this environment may be ill prepared to spend time on learning tasks in the classroom. Confusion abounds, stemming from a lack of intellectual skills and content mastery.

CHANGING REALITIES

In the mid-1960s America's community colleges proliferated, as each year spawned new institutions to accommodate the baby boom generation (Roeuche and Baker 1987). A new faculty signed on to teach these burgeoning numbers of students. Typical faculty members, fresh from graduate school, were in their late twenties or early thirties.

As the community colleges enter the 21st century, many of these same faculty members remain on staff. Among them are some of higher education's most innovative, motivated teachers. Yet, despite the enthusiasm, there is a pervasive sense that something different from the traditional must be done to teach students. This desire to change stems not from despair or weariness but from a mature assessment of what is required to facilitate learning in today's student.

Over the years, many scholars have identified a mix of these three attributes in good teachers:

◆ content mastery

◆ personal authenticity

◆ knowledge of how to teach

Presumably, nothing has altered the faculty's need to master subject matter or to be a person of integrity. The changed factor for good teaching stems from what "how to teach" requires today.

In the past, the lecture method may have been sufficient as a tool for good teaching. Students of three decades ago had a relative similarity of life and school experience. Many of the students of 30 years ago came from homes where no television reigned. They all typically brought skills in reading and writing, which enabled them to be successful in college. A slower pace of life prevailed. With that slower pace, attention to the spoken word and passive listening received value in the culture. The work world of the mid-1960s also placed value on the assembly line, a hierarchical division of labor. Passive listening to an authority figure lecturing prepared the students of yesterday for the realities of the workforce (Meyers 1991). Today, students bring less commonality with them to college from their life and schooling. The range of life experience and academic skills is so diverse that a variety of teaching pedagogies is needed if this spectrum of students is to learn effectively.

The changes brought by technology and global competition have undermined the desirability of passivity in America's workers. The pace of life accelerated with the television, the automobile, the airplane, and the computer. Visual, fast-paced communication became the norm. Attention spans shortened. With these developments, lectures became less productive for audiences. "Watching a lecture" paralleled "watching television." Many students judged the worth of a lecture on its entertainment value. By the mid-1990s, thinking and communication skills outranked an obedient disposition. These changing realities in college teaching point to the need for active learning strategies for students.

FACULTY RESPONSE TO CHALLENGES

To improve teaching and learning requires innovation in assisting individual students and faculty to do better. Although a certain artistry is involved in the dynamics between teacher and student, skills in teaching well can be shared and developed. Faculty development, at its best, can assist faculty in examining and sharing what works and what does not in teaching and learning.

To pursue the creation of faculty development aimed at improving teaching and learning, colleges should strive for the following three characteristics:

- communal collaboration among faculty over a sustained time

- specific, focused attempts at improving the learning in disciplinary courses

- concentrated efforts to ascertain how well students are learning throughout a course

It is hoped that these three characteristics will provide the context for implementing the active learning strategies provided in this book.

The first characteristic contains three noteworthy elements. "Collaboration" with others in a community with a shared interest creates a framework for responsibility, intellectual stimulation, and creativity. The reality of the "faculty" community implies a group of teaching practitioners who are willing to share from their real teaching life. And "over a sustained time" recognizes the importance of the process of teaching and learning. Meaningful teaching-improvement projects require the development, implementation, and assessment of the improvement effort, which requires sustained effort over time.

The second characteristic recognizes that teaching well means teaching well in a specific context—the disciplinary context. This recognition brings intellectual credibility to faculty development by grounding improvement efforts in the mental constructs of the disciplines. In addition, by targeting the "improving of learning," the emphasis is on assisting the student, emphasizing what the student does in order to learn better.

The third characteristic of faculty development aimed at improving teaching and learning involves at least three different elements. First, it involves the obvious issue of mastery of the subject matter. This is the traditional domain covered by tests and assignments. The second element involves the student's reflection on how well the subject matter is mastered. This element can involve analysis of both the faculty member and student's role in the teaching-learning process. The third element involves metacognition on the student's part—thinking about how one thinks.

The above three characteristics of faculty development aimed at improving teaching and learning can be structured by a college or university, a department or division, or by a system or consortium. Ultimately, however, each faculty member must own the improvement of teaching and learning as his or her responsibility. Faculty evolution and development fit into a personal profile of the faculty member as teacher-learner.

Fostering Critical Thinking through Writing and Speaking Strategies

This book rests on four central assumptions about critical thinking, college education, teaching, and learning:

♦ Teaching students to think well is the primary obligation of college faculty.

♦ Students must be challenged to move beyond recall and comprehension to the intellectual skills that more properly constitute critical thinking.

♦ Students develop critical thinking skills through practice in structured active learning strategies in which they write and speak.

♦ Faculty can learn how to teach thinking through sharing active learning strategies with each other.

TEACHING STUDENTS TO THINK WELL

College faculty have two primary goals in their teaching. One is to ensure that students acquire organized knowledge, information, and facts; the other is to develop thinking skills in students. The two goals are intertwined. The development of thinking skills depends on thinking about something, but gaining and comprehending information, though necessary, is insufficient in an education. Deepening one's knowledge and one's thinking ability should grow in tandem.

Within the academic community, there is a debate over the best way to teach thinking to students. Should there be separate courses in "thinking" or "critical thinking"? Within the disciplinary courses, how overtly should thinking be taught? While the arguments on either side of these questions have merit, this book adopts the perspective that faculty need to teach thinking explicitly across the curriculum. Of the two goals, knowledge acquisition and thinking skills, the goal of teaching thinking skills—teaching students to think well—is the more crucial to achieving college-level learning.

CHALLENGING STUDENTS TO MOVE BEYOND RECALL

The identification, recall, and comprehension of information is necessary and appropriate, but it is insufficient to achieve the goal of thinking. The thinking process in college occurs primarily in the context of academic disciplines. Students must be challenged to move beyond the memorization function to the intellectual skills that more properly define thinking. Students in any part of the curriculum must be exposed to the central information, ideas, and facts of a given discipline; at the same time they must be able to engage in the "higher order" thinking abilities.

Benjamin Bloom's *Taxonomy* (1956) provides a schemata on the variety of intellectual skills, from the simple levels to the more complex. Here are the basic components of his theory of thinking:

♦ RECALL of information, description

♦ COMPREHENSION and retention of central facts, ideas

♦ APPLICATION of principles and ideas to information

♦ ANALYSIS by probing into information with ideas, principles; finding evidence for conclusions

♦ SYNTHESIS by combining ideas into a new whole, creatively changing ideas and principles

♦ EVALUATION of decisions, judgments, thinking by using criteria

When students move beyond recall and comprehension to application, analysis, synthesis, and evaluation, they become critical thinkers.

Many such models focus on what it means to think well. Richard Paul in *Critical Thinking: Educational Imperative* (Barnes 1992) defines critical thinking as disciplined, self-directed thinking that exemplifies the perfections of thinking appropriate to a particular model or domain of thought. Paul classifies thought in terms of its perfections and imperfections, as shown in Table 1.1.

Table 1.1 Perfections and Imperfections of Thought

Perfections	Imperfections
Clarity	Unclarity
Precision	Imprecision
Specificity	Vagueness
Accuracy	Inaccuracy
Relevance	Irrelevance
Consistency	Inconsistency
Logicalness	Illogicalness
Depth	Superficiality
Completeness	Incompleteness
Significance	Triviality
Fairness	Bias
Adequacy (*for purpose*)	Inadequacy

In *Teaching Thinking: Issues and Approaches* (1990), Robert J. Schwartz and David N. Perkins give another perspective. They classify three types of thinking, with some of the core skills generated by each category (*see Table 1.2*).

For John Chaffee in *Critical Thinking: Educational Imperative* (Barnes 1992), thinking generally refers to a variety of complex, cognitive activities such as

- solving problems
- generating and organizing ideas
- forming and applying concepts
- designing systematic plans of action
- constructing and evaluating arguments
- exploring issues from multiple perspectives
- applying knowledge to new situations

- critically evaluating the logic and validity of information
- developing evidence to support views
- carefully analyzing situations
- discussing subjects in an organized way

Joel Peterson develops a model of good thinking in "Twenty-Three Skills and Dispositions of Effective Thinking Targeted for Curricular Emphasis in the Minnesota Community College System" (1994). Based on his work, funded by a statewide critical thinking grant in Minnesota's community colleges, Peterson formulates the Thinking F.I.R.E. model:

Factual Thinking (F)

This function involves the observation and recall of details, encompassing concrete external facts as well

Table 1.2 Three Types of Thinking

Useful Retention of Ideas	Generation of Ideas	Assessment of Ideas
Classification/definition	Multiplicity of ideas	Finding reasons/ conclusions
Comparing/contrasting	Varied ideas	Finding assumptions
Parts/whole	Novel ideas	Accurate observation
Ordering ideas	Elaborated ideas	Reliable sources
Pattern recognition	Composition of ideas	Causal explanation
Relation to previous knowledge	Challenging assumptions	Prediction
		Generalization
		Analogy
		Conditional reasoning

as internal subjective experiences. Instruction that focuses on factual thinking aims at developing a mind trained to care about details, seek out patterns, and recall facts with accuracy and completeness.

Insightful Thinking (I)

This function involves taking what is present as also having hidden dimensions and potentials. It involves awareness of what could be, could have been, or could come to be. It is often expressed through symbol or story. Instruction focused on insightful thinking aims at developing a mind that pushes toward hidden possibilities, toward more encompassing perspectives, and toward symbolic expression.

Rational Thinking (R)

This function concerns the objective relations between the elements that are perceived. Rational thinking puts the given into conceptual order by finding or creating logical connections between different ideas and facts. Instruction focused on rational thinking aims at developing a mind that seeks order through identifying, testing, and applying abstract relations, structures, and processes.

Evaluative Thinking (E)

This thinking function involves recognizing and expressing the value we give to perceived facts and possibilities, making explicit our feelings of attraction or repulsion in relation to issues at hand. Instruction focused on evaluative thinking aims at developing a mind that gives voice to its own value responses, considers other views objectively, and commits to the view it feels is best.

Although the models have characteristics that distinguish them from one another, they are more notable for the characteristics and critical thinking abilities they share. Table 1.3 shows common threads found in more than one critical thinking model.

Table 1.3 Common Threads in Critical Thinking Models

Assessment of Ideas	Generation, Creation of Ideas
Assumptions; identifying issues	Insight
Evidence; sufficiency	Point of view; other perspectives
Observation; perceiving facts, data	Synthesis
Conclusions; finding reasons	Hypothesis
Analysis	
Consequences; seeing implications	
Distinctions; finding relevance, consistency	
Problem solving	

In addition, any of these elements can be done well or poorly.

Moving beyond Lecture

Distinguishing critical thinking from the factual content in a course, as well as defining critical thinking, makes for a good foundation for learning. It does not resolve the tension that exists between emphasizing critical thinking and covering the course content, however. One of the most common objections of faculty to engaging in activities that promote critical thinking is the belief that they already have "too much material to cover."

This defense of the need to cover course content often begs the question of whether substantial student learning is occurring. Often, a total emphasis on coverage results in short-term retention of disparate facts at the expense of understanding. It is therefore essential to recognize that a balance between thinking and course content is necessary.

Recent research illustrates the limits of lecturing. In *Promoting Active Learning* (1993, 14–15), Chet Meyers and Thomas B. Jones summarize some of this research:

- While teachers are lecturing, students are not attending to what is being said 40 percent of the time.

- In the first 10 minutes of lecture, students retain 70 percent of the information; in the last 10 minutes, 20 percent.

- Four months after taking an introductory psychology course, students knew only 8 percent more than a control group who had never taken the course.

This is not to suggest the elimination of the lecture, but rather a diminished, restructured role for it. If students are relatively attentive for 10 minutes, then 10-minute mini-lectures used in tandem with other strategies may be more appropriate to the learning process.

The need to change teaching pedagogies stems not only from research on learning theory but also from a realization that students need to learn more than course content. A fundamental need exists for students to be taught how to think, not what to think. Learning involves thinking in order to gain knowledge. The identity of a learned person involves one whose mind creates principles, strategies, insights, and concepts—not facts. "Talking at" someone rarely conveys the knowledge of principles, strategies, concepts, facts, or insight at a sufficient level. This can be done only through student response and responsibility for becoming a thinker.

At the core of thinking well is the mastery of four intellectual skills—listening, speaking, reading, and writing (as well as other symbol making). Faculty need to create learning activities in which listening is supplemented by writing, speaking, and reading. To do this, inquiry and questioning must be central.

Encouraging students to be active learners (critical readers, critical listeners, critical writers, and critical speakers) requires greater depth and less breadth in the curriculum. Persistent learning stems from in-depth experiences; the broadly based learning of facts is soon forgotten.

Students, through activities, must distinguish what they know from what they don't know. This involves an intellectual search for knowledge and values. In this process students need to create their own synthesis of knowledge while reflecting the standards of the intellectual life. These standards include precision, coherence, sufficiency, breadth, and accuracy.

In addition to drawing on faculty expertise, students need to draw on the knowledge base of other students to diminish what they do not know. Much student experience is rooted in misinformation, misconception, ignorance, bias, and prejudice. Active learning strategies, informed by critical thinking, are required to transform both students and faculty.

Although a definition of critical thinking is important and necessary, it is not enough to infuse thinking into the curriculum. When students embody the critical thinking abilities as defined, they become critical thinkers. They assume responsibility for their own thinking, including the implications and results of speaking and acting.

These thoughtful students explore ideas with reasonable, thorough questions. They gain a point of view but do not see their beliefs as identical with reality. These students exhibit a level of comfort with ambiguity and complexity and seek to reconcile contradictions. They are capable of generating and evaluating theories with accompanying reasons and evidence. Consideration of these characteristics leads to the issue of how students achieve critical thinking skills.

PRACTICING ACTIVE LEARNING STRATEGIES

The third assumption underlying this book is that students develop levels of thinking through active learning strategies.

Before faculty engage students in active learning strategies, they must be as explicit as possible about defining a model of critical thinking. Faculty should tell their students in the first class meeting about their goals and objectives relative to the thinking skills the students are expected to master. Handouts or audiovisual aids that emphasize this model of thinking abilities and skills are valuable. This model provides students with a vehicle for comprehending the purpose of the active learning strategies.

Faculty facilitate student development of critical thinking abilities and skills through active learning strategies, which put students into the role of thinkers primarily by engaging them in writing and speaking activities. Students also can develop intellectual skills by reading, listening, observing, calculating, and quantifying. Writing and speaking stand on higher ground than the other intellectual skills, because they are the two dominant ways people communicate their thinking.

By facilitating structured opportunities for students to write and speak, faculty assist students in developing a point of view and supporting it with adequate reasons. In this way students give birth to their own learning through the structured use of their minds. When faculty do develop student thinking through writing and speaking, they should articulate as clearly as possible their intention to build critical thinking through the activities.

In his book *The Paideia Proposal* (1982), Mortimer J. Adler examines three central dimensions of learning by describing their differing goals, means of attainment, and activities/operations.

Of particular note are the goals, means, and activities/operations in the development of intellectual skills and the skills of learning (*see Table 1.4, Column 2*). This column points out the learner's need to practice thinking in order to think well.

A central method of creating active learning activities for students is to intertwine knowledge acquisition with thinking to infuse critical thinking into the traditional curriculum. Good questions are the genesis of good thinking. Student responses to questioning can take many forms. The responses may be verbal or written, or both. Responses may be individual or in groups; they may occur in class or outside of class.

Two modes of student active response, writing and speaking, create thought. These two responses draw on two of the most dominant movements in higher education: writing across the curriculum and collaborative learning. Among other benefits, both movements have developed writing activities and small-group activities that promote thinking.

Active learning strategies also can encompass other movements of merit in higher education.

Table 1.4 Critical Thinking and the Multiple Dimensions of Learning

	Column 1	Column 2	Column 3
Goals	Acquisition of organized knowledge	Development of intellectual skills, skills of learning	Enlarged understanding of ideas and values
Means	*by means of* Didactic instruction, lectures and responses, textbooks, and other aids	*by means of* Coaching, exercises, and supervised practice	*by means of* Maieutic or Socratic questioning and active participation
Areas, Operations, and Activities	*in three areas of subject matter* Language, literature, and the fine arts Mathematics and natural sciences History, geography, and social studies	*in the operations of* Reading, writing, speaking, and listening Calculating, problem solving, observing, measuring, estimating Exercising critical judgment	*in the* Discussion of books (not textbooks) and other works of art, and involvement in artistic activities (e.g., music, drama, and visual arts)

Note: The three columns do not correspond to separate courses, nor is one kind of teaching and learning necessarily confined to any one class.

Multicultural diversity initiatives that explore class, race, and gender can benefit greatly from active learning strategies. Experiential, nontraditional, and adult learning all gain from a strategy to make students writers and speakers about their thinking. The classroom research/classroom assessment movement is grounded in a similar belief in feedback, in writing or speech, about the student's learning.

SHARING STRATEGIES TO TEACH THINKING

The fourth and final assumption is that faculty can best learn how to teach thinking through a specific case-study approach to active learning strategies. This assumption asserts that faculty can learn how to improve teaching from dialogue with peers and students, as well as from creative self-reflection.

Ernest L. Boyer, when asked about the characteristics of great teachers, responded:

> Great teachers of mine have had three characteristics. First, they know their subject matter. Secondly, they know a variety of techniques, they know how to teach. Finally, they are authentic, real people. This characteristic comes through in their teaching (1990).

The second characteristic that Boyer identifies—a variety of techniques, and knowing how to teach—can be learned by faculty. Teaching is a learned craft, not a genetic inheritance.

Unfortunately, American higher education has treated teaching (and by implication, learning) as a private domain. By extending the logic of academic freedom, faculty have moved away from public discussion and research about teaching and learning. Teaching and learning therefore need to become part of a communal conversation.

Teaching Thinking

While discourse about teaching and learning needs to focus on a variety of topics (great teachers of mine, what I valued as a student, critical moments in my life as a teacher, memorable students), the central topic must be on what works to generate student learning and what does not.

The basis for a teaching transformation among college faculty can be summarized in the following:

♦ Speak less so students do and think more.

♦ Develop specific strategies and activities for the facilitation of student thinking.

The first suggestion involves shifting the focus of course activity from the faculty to the students. Time and again, longitudinal studies of student learning affirm the value of engaged, active learning for students and the progressive diminution of learning through lectures. The implication of this research is for faculty to transform their teaching by using short blocks of time to give information or to extract and organize information provided by students.

The two most obvious methods of replacing lecture time in the classroom are

♦ student writing-reading activities

♦ student speaking-listening activities

From these activities faculty can draw on student conclusions to inform their speech in the classroom. Socratic exchange, a type of speech exercise in which students respond to questions posed for them by faculty, works well after students have engaged the material through writing and speaking with other students. The teaching faculty might replace information giving with activities that encourage thinking aloud and modeling critical thinking.

The second piece of advice urges faculty to develop specific, focused strategies and activities designed to promote student thinking. In the attempt to probe topics more thoughtfully and in greater depth, faculty can use regular writing in a variety of formats and small-group work to provide the central structure.

All these activities, as well as assignments completed outside the classroom, need to focus on the thinking process. The instructor might require portfolios of all student written work to collect the thinking of the student, practice sample grading to keep the task manageable, and let small-group work be processed into writing exercises for the portfolios. Well-structured activities permit faculty to call on students randomly and to incorporate verbal exchanges into the grading as desired.

In all these activities, the thinking process should produce fundamental concepts with a high degree of generalization. The logic of the discipline needs to be central. Faculty must determine what the three or four central ideas of the course are from a disciplinary perspective. These concepts need to be made relevant through concrete examples. Real-life situations that illustrate the importance of "meaning making," problem solving, and goal setting are invaluable in creating learning. Pivotal in the information is the need for explicit intellectual standards for student grading.

In addition to this analysis of what student learning demands, it is important to look at faculty and their development process. While changes in the student body, the pace of life, and the workforce dictate a diminished role for the lecture, faculty members must be ready for the change.

Faculty Development

Individual faculty members will not change their behavior until they attain sufficient mastery of the course content to allow exploration beyond lecturing, and they become aware of models for creating a more active, thinking-oriented class.

Most faculty begin their teaching careers by attempting to organize the material of the course in a way that highlights important information. Initially, their concern is to cover the material in a factual manner. They are concerned about their credibility as college faculty and do not want to jeopardize it. As they continue in their teaching careers, they typically gain greater facility in their lectures. They find better anecdotes and more concrete illustrations. They use humor and stories to punctuate lectures and enhance the entertainment value.

Until they get to this point, faculty rarely will be willing to explore beyond the confines of lecturing. They need a certain level of comfort and security in dealing with the subject matter. They need to establish that as faculty they are not frauds or pretenders.

Once faculty reach this level of mastery and comfort, they typically need some sense of discontent to move to the next level. Often this discontent involves a sense of boredom with the repetition of the same subject matter again and again. Or it hinges on a sense that student learning is inadequate. Faculty realize the limits of mere information and of telling about that information, regardless of the interest level it generates. Part of the realization about the limits of lecturing and information comes from their inability to engage students in a serious way with these methods.

While vast numbers of college faculty wish to expand their teaching repertoire beyond lecturing and testing for recall of information, many are unaware of how to change teaching methods in a productive manner. They do not want student time and energy wasted in random, nondirected discussion. Nor do they want to read and grade vast quantities of subjective, opinionated student writing (White 1994). Faculty need access to proved active learning strategies that can enhance student thinking. They need to read, hear, and see models that have worked for other faculty. These examples should focus on what students do in various courses and how that student activity is directed toward the improvement of student thinking. Concrete, specific examples are a fine way to share knowledge about teaching. Case studies, which exemplify teaching methods, provide a fertile vehicle for learning about active learning strategies.

The speaking strategies can be achieved in collaborative, cooperative group work, in individual presentations, and in individual conferences between the faculty member and students. These speaking strategies can promote thinking through a variety of ways involving these variables:

- response to peer work
- pro–con debates
- problem solving
- role playing
- presentation of group projects
- individual/group projects doing the discipline
- formal or informal presentations
- graded or nongraded speaking

Speech can stand alone or it can be linked to writing. Writing, because of its deliberate nature, can provide a wonderful vehicle for thinking either within particular disciplines or in a more generic fashion. Writing can also be used for feedback, assessment, and self-assessment. Writing strategies can take a variety of forms:

- essay
- journal
- notes
- research
- lab work
- field work
- quiz, test
- in-class/out-of-class writing
- graded/nongraded writing

Case studies that share specific strategies for making students speakers and writers provide mod-

els for faculty to use as they deem appropriate in their own courses. Whereas some definitions of the case method focus on who is teaching what to whom and how, the case method in this volume refers primarily to how, and secondarily to what.

By integrating active learning strategies requiring students to speak and write, faculty move toward the implementation of a positive learning environment. Arthur Chickering and Zelda Gamson listed these items in their "Seven Principles for Good Practice in Undergraduate Education" (1990) as underlying good learning relationships between faculty and students:

- student-faculty contact
- active learning
- cooperation among students, among faculty
- time on task
- prompt feedback
- high expectations
- diverse ways of learning and teaching

Among these seven principles, active learning strategies stand as the centerpiece. Faculty can learn how to teach thinking and how to improve continually. Without it, faculty cannot fulfill their obligation to teach students to think well. Active learning is that principle, and strategy, through which faculty engage their students in thinking.

Critical Thinking in the Social Sciences

Within the community of theoreticians on critical thinking are those who argue that critical thinking should not be characterized generically, as was done with the definitions in chapter 1. They argue that critical thinking can be understood only from the perspective of the type of content or thought. In *Critical Thinking and Education*, John McPeck suggests this approach:

> It is a matter of conceptual truth that thinking is always *thinking about X*, and that *X* can never be "everything in general" but must always be something in particular. Thus the claim "I teach students to think" is at worst false and at best misleading. . . . In isolation from a particular subject, the phrase "critical thinking" neither refers to nor denotes any particular skill. It follows from this that it makes no sense to talk about critical thinking as a distinct subject and that it therefore cannot profitably be taught as such. To the extent that critical thinking is not about a specific sub-ject *X*, it is both conceptually and practi-cally empty. The statement "I teach critical thinking," *simpliciter*, is vacuous because there is no generalized skill properly called critical thinking (1981, 4–5).

Although this argument has been used to crit-icize separate, stand-alone approaches of teaching critical thinking, the ideas in the quotation may be used to make another point. Although "thinking is always thinking about *X*" and specific background knowledge is essential for critical thinking in a par-ticular area, for the purposes of this book a "par-ticular subject" is defined broadly as the academic discipline or division of the social sciences. Although the social science point of view consti-tutes a variation in what counts for good, effective thinking compared with the humanities, sciences, and professional-occupational education, the sim-ilarities outweigh the differences. A full under-standing of a discipline, field, or area requires the ability to think critically in that field, but the abil-ity to think critically in one field has transfer capacity for thinking critically in others.

When examining what it means for an anthropologist, a psychologist, an economist, a sociologist, a political scientist, a geographer, or a historian to think well in these disciplines, it is helpful to examine a definition of "habits of the mind" used by effective social scientists.

Over a two-year period from 1991 to 1993, faculty in Minnesota's community colleges grappled with the question of what it means to "think well" in their particular discipline. The following definition includes those elements specified by faculty in many disciplines. Discipline-based groups within the social sciences identified 23 thinking skills and dispositions to emphasize in social-science courses.

As faculty identified these 23 key skills and dispositions, they classified them into one of four categories of thinking: thinking concerned with facts; thinking concerned with insight; thinking concerned with reasoning; and thinking concerned with values.

Table 2.1 shows their checklist of "habits of the

Table 2.1 Checklist of Habits of Mind for Effective Thinking

Factual Thinking— Detailed Thinking Concerning Observations and Factual Claims	Insightful Thinking— "Big Picture" Thinking That Draws on Insight and Imagination	Rational Thinking— Logical Thinking Focused on Reasoning and Structure	Evaluative Thinking
◆ Factual clarity, accuracy, and fairness ◆ Observational detail, reliability, and scope ◆ Effective recording and recall strategies ◆ Alertness for patterns	◆ Seeking the larger context ◆ Seeking alternative perspectives ◆ Relating the known to the unknown ◆ Using questions as probes ◆ Applying learning to self-understanding ◆ Deriving lessons from experiences	◆ Identifying structure and order ◆ Formulating hierarchies and rules governing patterns ◆ Identifying and evaluating arguments ◆ Constructing arguments ◆ Working with rules to reach goals ◆ Judging strength of evidence ◆ Awareness of thinking strategies (metacognition)	◆ Reflective thinking that draws out underlying values and feelings ◆ Sensitivity to values—individual and collective ◆ Applying values to problems ◆ Respect for individual and collective differences ◆ Willingness to risk and commit ◆ Valuing individual and collective self

mind" for effective thinking defined by category.

Faculty across the social sciences initially affirmed these skills and dispositions, as did faculty teaching in the humanities, science and mathematics, and professional-occupational programs. Then, faculty in all these curricular areas reexamined the items. In the reexamination, they eliminated some items as less important than others. They also added subcategories to amplify the disciplinary meanings of the skills and dispositions.

Social science faculty dropped two items as less important: "relating the known to the unknown" (Insightful Thinking) and "working with rules to reach goals" (Rational Thinking).

For the remaining items, the social science faculty added subclassifications. Following is that more detailed list of critical thinking abilities and skills in the social sciences:

I. Factual Thinking: Thinking Concerned with the Gathering of Factual Information Relevant to an Issue or Problem

A. To seek out relevant facts and factual claims with concern for clarity, accuracy, and fairness
 1. To master methods of research useful for ensuring the fair, balanced, and accurate and efficient gathering of facts
    a) To master strategies of reading that help raise questions of the reliability, precision, and balance of the factual claims presented or assumed
    b) To master methods useful for critically analyzing standardized report forms such as research reports, etc.
    c) To master methods of efficient library research
 2. To distinguish fact from opinion, interpretation, or assumption
    a) In observation, listening, and reading

b) In reading graphs, tables, charts, etc.
 3. To raise questions to clarify ambiguity, vagueness, and confusion in terminology, concepts, and observations
 4. To question and judge the accuracy, reliability, and balance of factual claims; to seek disconfirming evidence and suppressed evidence as well as confirming evidence

B. To make perceptive observations that are detailed, accurate, comprehensive, and conscious of their limitations
 1. To develop a vocabulary useful for focusing and recording observations
 2. To make observations with metacognitive awareness of criteria and the potential for bias, gaps, inconsistencies, ambiguities, assumptions
    a) To take into account the increased likelihood of bias in particular areas of sensitivity, such as politics, religion, ethnicity, gender, privilege, and responsibility
 3. To master methods useful for accurate detailed recording of observations
    a) Methods for controlling variables, changing one variable at a time
    b) Quantitative observation strategies
    c) Qualitative observation strategies
    d) Use of notes, charts, diagrams, tables, grids, etc.
 4. To seek out conflicting as well as corroborating observations, to check the replicability of the observations, and to minimize the influence of the observer on the observations
 5. To consider and judge ethical issues that may be involved in observing, collecting, and using factual information
 6. To recognize subjective as well as objective observational data, and to recognize the relevance of subjective information to comprehensive information

C. To master and apply strategies for efficient recording and recall of factual information

   1. To use mnemonic devices

   2. To keep good notes, records, and visual displays (such as diagrams, graphs, charts, etc.) to organize observations and facts for easy recall

   3. To master word-roots helpful to aid in the recall of vocabulary

D. To seek out and identify patterns in observed and reported factual data

   1. To ask habitually, Is there a pattern here?

   2. To develop vocabulary that increases consciousness of patterns and the ability to identify them

   3. To develop mastery of methods useful for identifying and testing patterns, e.g.:

     a) The use of tables and charts to array information to make patterns more visible

     b) The use of methods of agreement, difference, and concomitant correlation for formulating and testing hypotheses to explain patterns

     c) The use of predictions based on extrapolation or interpolation to test hypotheses

   4. To use patterns to improve performance, e.g., the use of "classic moves" in argument, etc.

II. Imaginative Thinking: Thinking That Seeks Insightful and Creative Representations of Wholes and Parts

A. To identify encompassing frameworks (such as theories, purposes, systems, dynamics of change, interpretations, or world views) that give significance to facts and relations by situating them within larger perspectives

   1. To seek to expand one's perspective on observed facts in order to see the facts in a new light, as part of some larger whole, e.g.:

     a) To understand facts and events in historical or personal developmental perspective—in relation to what was, what is, and what could be in the future

     b) To understand the concrete individual or event in relation to the abstract general rules, theories, or systems

     c) To understand the individual in relation to the collective, the cultural, the economic, the species, the biosphere, the cosmos, etc.

   2. To be able to construct models, theories, analogies, metaphors, stories, etc., to construct explanations of facts, events, and relations

   3. To be able to articulate the strengths and weaknesses of alternative explanatory models, theories, analogies, etc., and of alternative forms of evidence

   4. To be able to use models, theories, analogies, etc., to help distinguish useful from nonuseful factual information

B. To go beyond the frameworks that are commonplace and come most readily to mind, to find opposing or alternative frameworks

   1. To compare and contrast alternative explanations, options, hypotheses, etc.

     a) To evaluate the limitations and relative adequacy of alternative explanatory frameworks

     b) To develop a more complete understanding of your habitual framework and its assumptions in relation to other frameworks

C. To seek imaginative ways to use ideas in alternative modes and media

   1. To be able to use techniques for encouraging imaginative thinking (e.g., brainstorming, synectics)

2. To be able to express or understand an idea, or a set of relations analogously, e.g.:
   a) Through metaphor, imagery, and symbolism
   b) Through stories
   c) Through artistic creation
3. To be able to express an idea or a set of relations concretely or abstractly
4. To be able to express an idea or a set of relations through associations of feelings and images
5. To be able to express an idea or a set of relations through thought experiments
6. To be able to express an idea or a set of relations by relating them to everyday situations or to imagined contexts

D. To develop the art of asking questions to probe obscurities and explore alternatives
   1. To develop habits of active listening and reading, and to exhibit an active imagination and curiosity
   2. To use questions to clarify impreciseness
   3. To use questions to identify gaps in what is known
   4. To use questions to identify hidden agendas
   5. To use questions to identify anomalies
   6. To use questions to identify limitations in models, theories, explanations, etc.
   7. To use questions to probe consequences: If that, then what? or What if . . .?

E. To relate learning to developing a more complete sense of self-understanding
   1. To ask, as alternative ways of thinking, understanding, and communicating are discovered, Why do I believe the way I do? Why do I believe as I do?
   2. To examine thoughts and actions for the possibility of bias, self-deception, and hidden agendas

F. To reflect on successful and unsuccessful experiences alike, in order to improve thinking and self-understanding
   1. To reflect on the strengths and weaknesses of thinking strategies in successful and unsuccessful experiences alike, and to formulate or revise norms for handling similar situations in the future
   2. To practice error analysis on performance, in order to discover patterns that can then be addressed

III. Rational Thinking: Thinking Concerned with Identifying or Applying Logical Structures, Sequences, Rules, Strategies, etc.

A. To identify in a natural or created thing the structure, sequence, or dynamics by which it is organized
   1. To be able to identify fundamental schemata and modes of discourse in common use and in academic use (e.g., comparison/contrast, problem and solution, critique and propose)
   2. To seek out, identify, and test cause-and-effect relations, including cases with multiple causalities

B. To be able to identify or formulate hierarchical structures—including hierarchies of abstraction or generalization—and to articulate relations between items on different levels
   1. To be able to group and categorize in order to reduce data to comprehensible sets and relations
   2. To be able to formulate group properties and relationships between things on different hierarchical levels, e.g., relationships between the individual, collective, and societal attributes, relationships between claims about the macro- and microlevels of analysis

3. To be able to grasp abstract claims and give concrete examples; to be able to relate lab work, case studies, and personal experiences to abstract theories presented in readings and lectures

4. To be able to make inferences about concrete experiences from data displayed on charts, graphs, diagrams, etc.

5. To be able to test generalizations and hypotheses on the basis of factual evidence using basic principles of statistical significance

C. To be able to identify, analyze, and evaluate arguments implicit or explicit in the claims of others

1. To be able to recognize and evaluate explicit or implicit premises, including assumptions

2. To be able to analyze and evaluate the relevance of evidential claims to an argument's conclusion

3. To be able to evaluate the validity or relative strength of an argument's logical deductions and implications

4. To be able to recognize and articulate explicit or implicit conclusions

   a) To be able to distinguish basic logical types of relationships between evidence and conclusions (e.g., deductive certainty, inductive and statistical probability, indirect proof, support or counterevidence for a hypothesis, etc.)

   b) To be able to identify common fallacies —argument forms with strong psychological appeal but minimal inductive strength

5. To be able to evaluate competing hypotheses, e.g., in terms of explanatory power, burden of proof, crucial experiment, disconfirmability, etc.

D. To be able to create clear, cogent arguments using reliable factual evidence to support a view or reach a conclusion

1. To seek and offer reasons for your positions

2. To identify and articulate assumptions

3. To use and test deductions, inductions, and hypotheses

4. To identify and use essential information and claims, and to set aside nonrelevant information and claims

E. To develop the ability to recognize when evidence and logic warrants taking a position, changing a position, or withholding judgment

F. To increase self-awareness of thinking strategies, expand repertoire, and develop expertise at choosing among them

1. To develop metacognition—thinking about thinking while thinking about the task at hand

2. To develop a repertoire of thinking strategies, an awareness of their strengths and weaknesses for various tasks, and the ability to choose well among them (e.g., working backwards, seeking analogous problems, analyzing the problem into subproblems)

3. To be able to choose between and use appropriate technology for working on a problem, and to be able to devise applications of technology to meet the needs presented by a problem

4. To be able to choose a rhetorical structure that is effective in relation to the audience and the goals you wish to achieve

5. To be able to prioritize items in efficient, logical sequence or in order of importance

6. To be able to sequence questions for efficient and effective probing for information

IV. Evaluative Thinking: Thinking That Recognizes and Brings to Bear Value Considerations in Questions of What to Believe or Do

A. To recognize value positions inherent in the views of others and yourself, and to develop expertise in dealing with them
1. To be able to discern the important from the unimportant, the beneficial from the harmful, the high priority from the low priority, etc., from your own value framework and also from the value frameworks of others
2. To recognize value-related limitations on what you (or others) will do or believe
3. To recognize and demythologize cultural values related to power, race, and gender
4. To recognize the values that shape particular cultures, including the cultures of various academic disciplines and occupational fields
5. To put in context problems, decisions, discussions, etc., so that efforts are sensitive to the values of those concerned

B. To evaluate proposals, actions, products, and beliefs in relation to your own values and also in relation to cultural and group values; to evaluate actions and products in relation to quantifiable indices, when appropriate

C. To respect and value diversity in thinking processes and perspectives
1. To seek to identify and understand differences in assumptions, thinking patterns, values, feelings, etc.
2. To recognize the advantages of being open to and willing to learn the views of others who come from differing backgrounds and different life experiences
3. To understand the roots and role of intolerance in and between social groups
4. To be able to think suppositionally—in other words, to be able to consider and reason from assumptions and positions with which you disagree
5. To be able to work effectively in collaborative groups—to contribute to the sense of community as well as to the solution of problems, and to be capable of giving and receiving support
6. To be capable of giving and receiving constructive criticism aimed at improving the work, not at devaluing the person

D. To be willing to take risks and make commitments, while acknowledging and putting into perspective fears of criticism or failure
1. To be able to assume risks, which can include:
   a) Being wrong
   b) Finding and speaking in your own voice
   c) Committing ideas to writing
   d) Taking on complex issues and problems
   e) Challenging authorities and received opinion
   f) Making personal and social changes
   g) Learning to use new technology
   h) Changing your position when warranted by counterevidence and counterarguments
2. To be able to use criticism positively for improving work, without feeling threatened

E. To value yourself, your thoughts, and your feelings, while seeking to improve your work, learning, and self-awareness
1. To seek awareness of your own beliefs, values, and habits of thought—and their relationships to collective beliefs, values, and habits of thought—and to have the courage to articulate them, although it may seem risky
2. To develop an "I can be successful" attitude, including self-disciplined habits of managing time well and following through on tasks

3. To understand the self as a being in process, and to recognize weaknesses and strengths in your knowledge and abilities as opportunities for self-development rather than as threats to your ego

4. To seek to identify the significance for self-development and collective enrichment conveyed by feelings such as fear, performance anxiety, etc.

5. To value the self-improvement and collective enrichment that occurs through the mastery of basic abilities and concepts, the refinement of one's work, and the desire to learn

These are the critical thinking abilities and skills that the active learning strategies in subsequent chapters intend to develop. The active learning strategies are not activity for activity's sake but rather are directed at enhancing critical thinking abilities and skills.

CHAPTER THREE

Writing in the Disciplines: Fostering Critical Thinking

Writing is the process through which the product of thinking becomes visible. Thought gains a characteristic of sustainability through writing, which makes thought available into the future and to others besides the thinker. The process of hand, eye, and brain activity causes the writer to choose and commit to symbols of thinking.

Writing is valuable in the education process for several reasons. Writing helps students to process and sort information in order to create coherent knowledge for themselves. Writing allows the faculty member to learn the thinking process of the student. And writing allows students to share their thinking with one another.

Developing thinking skills is analogous to developing motor skills. Both types of skill demand regular use and practice. Writing, along with speaking, is a central method of developing one's thinking. Writing needs to be regular and ongoing to develop thinking; it can be done in class and outside of class, and can be graded or ungraded.

To draw the connection between writing and thinking, faculty must ask good questions. The

Figure 3.1 Reasons to Write

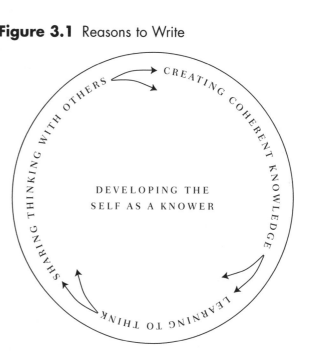

CREATING COHERENT KNOWLEDGE

THINKING WITH OTHERS

SHARING THINKING WITH OTHERS

DEVELOPING THE SELF AS A KNOWER

LEARNING TO THINK

formulation of the writing assignment by the faculty member should be clear in its intent to elicit the best in student writing and thinking. Drawing the connection between writing and thinking can be clarified by examining the process and elements of both.

The process of writing has several elements. Initially, a writer must be committed enough to the writing itself to do it. Before actually composing the ideas in words, a writer begins by searching and sorting through information pertinent to the topic. This information-gathering process can take on many forms, from memory and brainstorming to interviewing and library research. In the process of writing, the writer often discovers her or his own thoughts and feelings on the topic at hand. This discovery is termed finding one's voice. The precision and depth of thoughts and feelings are often attained through revising and editing.

Chapter 1 offered several theoretical models of the elements and process of thinking. Table 3.1 (*far right*) shows a functional model.

For use within the academic disciplines, the questions listed in "The Elements of Reasoning within a Point of View" provide a foundation for helping students explore thinking through writing.

In the introductory part of a course, faculty may find it helpful to preface these elements of thinking with a more basic activity, such as a written exercise to summarize information and identify key terms and concepts. This type of basic writing and thinking can provide the foundation for the sophistication students need to reason: analysis, comparison–contrast, argumentation, application, problem-solving, and evaluation.

When faculty design writing assignments for students in the discipline, they need to blend the process and the elements of writing and thinking. Here are some ideas to keep in mind when designing assignments:

◆ Use the important concepts and ideas of thinking within the discipline.

◆ Create optional questions that allow the student some variety of response.

◆ Clarify for yourself exactly why you think this piece of writing is important.

◆ Convey, in writing if possible, to the students why it is important.

◆ Create an audience, other than yourself, for the writing and make the ideas matter to that audience.

In addition, different types of writing give students practice at the intellectual skill of thinking. While it is important to continue the formal, graded papers and essay tests, additional possibilities can be helpful in providing students with practice in writing and thinking:

◆ "Short writes" or "five-minute writes." These provide a vehicle for in-class, ungraded writing. They stimulate student thinking and discussion. The same idea of brevity can translate to one-page, outside-of-class writing exercises.

◆ Question generation. Students generate two or three questions from an assigned reading.

◆ Journal.

These examples illustrate writing activities designed to stimulate thinking and learning. Often they are exploratory, unedited, and ungraded. These written activities may be assembled within a student portfolio that contains all student writing.

Within the academic disciplines, the concepts of tradition and innovation tie to "thinking well." In most disciplines, thinking well involves students going beyond self-expression and sharing their own voice. It involves engaging in thinking from the perspective of that discipline. Written assignments, graded or ungraded, in class or outside of class, can develop student thinking in that discipline.

Table 3.1 The Elements of Reasoning within a Point of View

	Assumptions within a Point of View What is the issue? What assumptions are built into the reasons? What would one have to do to settle the issue?	**Look Behind** Deep assumption
	concepts	
Other Evidence, Reasons, Data, Information What other evidence is pertinent to the reasoning?	Evidence, reasons, data, Information Sufficient? Acceptable? Relevant?	**Look to the Other Side** **Other Points of View**
	concepts/inference	
Look to One Side	**Solution** **Conclusion** **Interpretation**	**Other Positions** What other positions have been taken? Have they been dealt with fairly?
Look Ahead	**Consequences** What will happen if the action or policy is implemented?	**Implications** What other positions is one committed to if one accepts the conclusion?

Note: This table is a modified version of a schema originally devised by Ralph J. Johnson with design and layout done by J. A. Blair.

The diagram in Figure 3.2 *(page 22)* by Lucy Cromwell, from *Critical Thinking: Educational Imperative* (Barnes 1992), offers a sense of how thinking skills function within the framework of an academic discipline.

Writing exercises can task students with exploring the range from general to specific knowledge within a given discipline in order to demonstrate their thinking.

The following numbered strategies, which make up the core of this book, focus on activities either written or spoken, designed to improve student thinking. These strategies rest on the assumption that intellectual skills in general, and thinking

Figure 3.2 Educators' Definitions of Disciplinary Frameworks

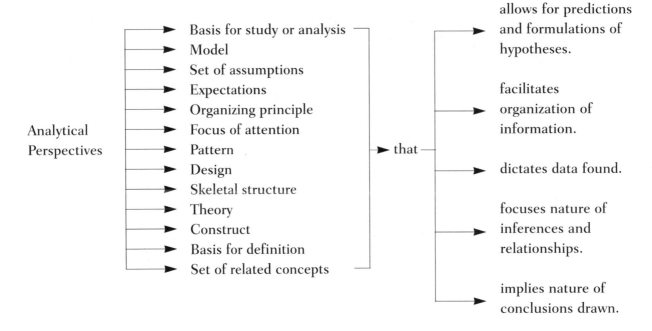

skills in particular disciplines, can improve only through practice and through feedback on those skills. This does not mean that student motivation and positive classroom climate are unimportant. If faculty are to shift from the role of lecturer and purveyor of the truth to one of coach and mentor, they must create a positive environment that encourages participation and risk taking. For the environment to succeed, students need to overcome their past socialization to passivity and become active in their learning.

GETTING STARTED

The best time to promote this model of active learning and participation is at the start of the course. Begin the course by emphasizing to students the worth of the discipline and the course. Personal stories and examples that demonstrate

passion for the course and teaching will help create the right climate. Self-disclosure in this regard helps create a bond between students and teacher.

Here are 11 activities for getting started in any social science course. They are intended to provide the opportunity for students to reflect on their background, approach, and responsibility for learning.

Warm-Ups

#1 *What Is a Good Course?*
At the start of a course, preferably on the first day, ask students to describe the elements in a good course. What is a good course? What is learning like at its best? How does teaching tie to learning at its best?

In addition, ask students to capture their idea of a good course and good learning in a metaphor or a drawing.

Have the students break into groups of three or four, introduce themselves, and share their writing and metaphors/drawings.

Process comments from a few of the groups.

#2 What Hinders Learning?

At the start of the course, ask students to identify in writing the social factors that create cultural ignorance. After a couple of minutes, ask them to identify social factors in their own life that hinder learning.

Have the students share the writings in small groups of three or four after personal introductions.

Have students discuss with each other how they might overcome one obstacle.

Process answers to any of the three activities as time permits.

#3 Writing on Day One

To create a sense of the importance of writing in the course, have students practice writing on the

Figure 3.3 Obstacles Hindering Learning

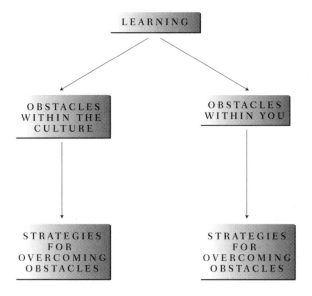

first day of class. In the last 15 minutes of the class session, ask them to write one page on the theme "What I Should Know about You." This could also be assigned for the next class meeting. This exercise can create a sense of linking the student to the faculty member and the course. It could also be used as the basis for an early conference between student and faculty.

#4 Another Approach: Writing (and Speaking) on Day One

Have students write a few sentences describing their worst experience in a class. Put students into small groups and have them talk about the experience and decide among themselves which experience was the worst. Have a volunteer (not necessarily the person who suffered through the event) then share the chosen story. The writing forces everyone in the class to take part in the activity to some extent, even if they write that they never had a negative experience in a class. This exercise seems to put students at ease when they discover that they are not alone in having fears.

#5 Before Day One: Structuring the Courses for Writing—Creating a Learning Community

While active teaching and learning strategies occur within individual courses, faculty should pay attention to creating a structure for students to encounter active strategies in two or more courses simultaneously. Paired courses, 12-credit packages, and sequenced offerings of paired or packaged courses can create a coherence in creating active learning among students. Spanning written assignments across more than one course and establishing discussion groups can assist students in developing their intellectual curiosity together. These efforts require a commitment of time, energy, and resources on the part of faculty and administrators, but the benefit to students can be substantial.

Examples of these innovative curricula are the learning communities at Evergreen Valley College, California; paired courses at La Guardia Community College, New York; and the College for Working Adults at Minneapolis Community College.

#6 *Setting the Tone: Day One*

The first day of class is crucial in establishing a community of learners. Faculty need to prepare for this day, to tell what is special about the course and to describe some of the course's possibilities. In the process it is important to show care for the students and to disclose something about oneself as the teacher. This helps create a unity and a sense of mutuality in the learning process.

To create a sense of mutuality, students need to be active and to share a bit. One way to get them involved is to put them in groups of four and ask them to share their names, something noteworthy about themselves personally, and their interest in college. Interrupt after six to eight minutes and tell the groups that they will each need to introduce themselves and one other person in the group with a piece of noteworthy information. (Introductions should take less than 30 seconds per person.) Give the groups an additional three or four minutes to finalize introductions.

This exercise helps break down barriers among students, and between students and faculty. A comfortable tone for learning can be created.

#7 *Structured Meetings Early in the Term with Individual Students during Office Hours*

During the first two or three weeks of the quarter, have students sign up for a 15-minute meeting during office hours. Before this meeting, have students write one to two pages on the following questions:

- What are my life goals? What do I want to achieve?
- What is the relationship of college to my life goals?
- What is the relationship of this course to my life goals?
- What strategies am I using?

Students should hand in their answers before the conference for reference in the discussion.

Students then need to prepare for the conference in a couple of ways. First, they are to come with two ideas to discuss. Second, they should identify two goals for the course.

By meeting the student in the first three to five weeks of the term, the faculty member can help retention and assist the student in becoming a committed learner.

#8 *Assessing Motivation and Commitment*

Have students begin the course by assessing their own motivation and commitment to higher education. Start this activity by asking the entire class to list ways to monitor motivation and commitment. Contrast this with a person lacking motivation and commitment.

Following the large-group discussion, have students write for five minutes on their own motivation and commitment. Ask them specifically to link these elements to that particular course. What are they committed to? Why are they motivated?

Discuss this writing in small groups of three or four students. In addition, have them identify how to improve motivation and commitment.

#9 *Student Goal Setting*

Before disseminating the course syllabus, ask students why they are in the course. What do they hope to gain from the course? How can you assist them in attaining those goals? Then link the answers to the syllabus with its goals, methods, and requirements.

#10 *Learning and Office Hours*

In the initial class session, ask students to write anonymous responses to tell you how they anticipate using your office hours. Have them respond to items like the following:

- Why are office hours available to students?

- Do you expect to use my office hours? How frequently?

- What would prevent your use of these office hours?

- What would help you to make productive use of these office hours?

Be sure to demonstrate your willingness to have students come and make use of the office hours.

#11 *Learning Strategies and Student Feedback*

At the start of a course, list all the strategies you could use to pursue the student learning objectives for the course. List them on a sheet and distribute it. A sample listing might include:

- structured lecture, loosely connected to the assigned reading

- summaries of the assigned reading

- short writing assignments outside of class

- short writing assignments in class

- small-group discussion of writing

- longer papers

- frequent exams

- two major tests

- group work as part of the grade

Ask students to choose two that would best promote their learning. Have them write why. Have them choose one strategy that they would not want used, and have them write why.

WRITING IN THE DISCIPLINES: FOSTERING CRITICAL THINKING

#12 *Critical Thinking Assignment*

Assignments that ask students to examine the evidence, assumptions, and reasoning in the disciplines create a potential for critical thinking. Here is an example of a critical thinking assignment in an American Studies course on Vietnam and America.

Finding the truth about Vietnam is at the core of "unwinding the Vietnam war" for Americans. The key question focuses on why the U.S. government went to war. Reasons for going to war are at the heart of whether a war is just. Below are 12 significant events in the development of American involvement in Vietnam. Choose at least four of these events.

Analyze each event using a three-step process:

1. State the interpretation of the event by the American government.

2. State the interpretation of the event by the Viet Minh Independence League and the Democratic Republic of Vietnam.

3. State your own evaluation based on the best reasoning and evidence.

Historic Events

1. After the departure of Japanese occupation forces, Ho Chi Minh and the Viet Minh Independence League established the Government of the Democratic Republic of Vietnam in Hanoi (September 2, 1945).

2. French troops returned to Vietnam (September 22, 1945).

3. The Viet Minh began an eight-year war against the French occupation with attacks in the north (December 19, 1946).

4. The United States announced it would provide military and economic aid to the French in Indochina, starting with a grant of $10 million (May 8, 1950).

5. The Viet Minh defeated the French at Dien Bien Phu (May 7, 1954).

6. The Geneva Agreements were signed, portioning Vietnam along the 17th Parallel and establishing an International Control Commission to supervise compliance (July 1954).

7. President Eisenhower and the United States advised Premier Ngo Dinh Diem that the country would provide assistance directly to South Vietnam rather than channeling aid through the French (October 24, 1954).

8. South Vietnam refused to participate in Vietnam-wide elections as called for in the Geneva Agreement on the grounds that elections would not be free in the north (July 20, 1955).

9. A U.S. military advisory group replaced French training of the South Vietnamese Army. The U.S.-supported government of Diem requested that the United States send military advisers (April 28, 1956).

10. President Kennedy dispatched 400 Special Forces soldiers and 100 additional military advisers, and authorized a campaign of clandestine warfare carried out by South Vietnamese personnel (May 11, 1961).

11. The U.S. Congress adopted the Tonkin Gulf Resolution endorsing measures needed to repel attack on American forces. This followed alleged attacks on the U.S. destroyers *Maddox* and *Turner Joy* by North Vietnamese torpedo boats (August 1964).

12. U.S. forces in Vietnam: (December 31, 1963)   16,300

    U.S. forces in Vietnam: (December 31, 1965)   185,300

    U.S. forces in Vietnam: (December 31, 1967)   465,000

    U.S. forces in Vietnam: (December 31, 1968)   536,000

    U.S. forces in Vietnam: (December 31, 1971)   156,800

    U.S. forces in Vietnam: (December 31, 1972)   24,200

#13 Analyzing a Historic Decision

To examine the crucial nature of critical thinking, select a pivotal historic decision. In a history class, this would enable students to understand how decisions are made.

For example, focus on the decision of Lyndon Johnson to deepen the American war in Vietnam. Have students read Johnson's speeches and view documentaries on his presidency. Ask them to identify the three central assumptions and the conclusions drawn historically. For another example, discuss Neville Chamberlain's reasons for deciding to sign the Munich Agreement with Hitler.

Were they accurate? If so, on what evidence do students judge their validity? If not, where is the error in thinking? What assumption and conclusion would have been more appropriate?

Assignments or in-class writing-discussions can be used to treat these questions.

#14 Five-Minute Writes

This strategy can be widely used for generating student thought on any subject. Formulate a question treating a significant topic in the course: Does this author have a view of evil? What is evil? Why is it considered evil? Is evil more than a matter of personal or cultural taste?

Give students five minutes to write their response to these questions. Help defuse anxiety by making disclaimers about the limits of the time period and the preliminary nature of the writing and tell students that the writing will not be collected. At the end of five minutes, put students in groups of three or four to discuss their writing and thinking. After six to 10 minutes, or whenever it feels like enough discussion has occurred, ask the students to come back to the class as a whole.

At this point, restate the original questions for the five-minute write. Ask for comments from the writing and discussion period. These comments from the students, when properly organized and supplemented, may well replace the lecture as a way of examining key questions.

In some courses, video materials exist that cover similar ground. For example, following the discussion on evil, a videotape of Bill Moyers interviewing Mortimer Allen on the nature of good and evil can add to the discussion. Often these video excerpts validate the insights of the students.

#15 *Fictional Autobiography in History: Portrait of a Native American Woman*
To put some substance into the multicultural orientation, have the students assume the character of a Native American woman and write about her life. This essay would fit well into either a history or a literature course. Structure the writing assignment so that it includes references to the historic, cultural reality and developments of the time period.

For example, in a course on American history after the Civil War, have students examine the life of a Sioux woman born in 1850. Describe the impact of contact with white traders, missionaries, and army. Trace her life through the Ghost Dance and the Wounded Knee massacre to life

on the reservation. While it is valuable to have students use their imagination, it is also important to have them ground this assignment in a historic context.

#16 *Historical Analysis*
After exploring a historic event for a number of weeks through readings and television documentaries, present students with a fictitious situation and ask them to form a judgment regarding its resolution. At the root of this exploration include some questions that relate to America's overall foreign policy toward developing nations. Student answers to the problem should reflect "an informed judgment," not simply a personal opinion. Have them consider historical precedent and the themes of foreign policy discussed in class.

Allow students to use notes while working on this exercise but not to discuss it with other classmates. Give students 20 minutes to complete the exercise.

In-Class Assignment
Suggest a hypothetical scenario: "The People's Republic of Marzipan, an emerging nation in Southeast Asia adjacent to Thailand, appears a likely candidate for a revolutionary upheaval. To date, the United States has supported the existing government, led by a minority landholding elite of the Protestant faith (and educated largely in England), with economic and small amounts of military aid. The majority of population is Hindu with strong ethnic ties to India. The main thrust of revolutionary activity comes from a peasant labor and agricultural union formed some 10 years ago by a revolutionary leader and his followers. His forces are likely to triumph in a military struggle. The People's Republic has some basic raw materials, a large population, and an as yet unexploited source of underground diamonds. The terrain of

Marzipan is very similar to areas the United States successfully fought in during World War II against the Japanese."

As a member of the National Security Council, you are asked to write a brief recommendation (the president doesn't like to read long reports) for an American foreign policy response. As the president has phrased it: "Can we afford to lose this country? What will happen if we don't take a stand here against an obviously radical political revolution?"

#17 Applying Rights Theory

Critical thinking often focuses on inductive reasoning—moving from specific facts to information and the assumptions and conclusions drawn from them. It also is important to have students explore deductive reasoning, moving from the general to the specific. Deductive reasoning exercises can be applied in constitutional legal history ethics, a legal studies curriculum, or a social issues course.

Have students read the Bill of Rights from the American constitution and discuss the documents in a general way. Then, pick a specific circumstance and have students apply a specific principle. For example, use the Fourth Amendment and the right to protection against unreasonable search and seizure. Have students apply this principle to drug testing. Ask them to respond to questions such as the following:

◆ Should drug testing of persons be permitted without reasonable suspicion?

◆ Should some occupations be tested regardless of suspicion? If so, which occupations? Police? Bus drivers? Pilots? Teachers? Doctors?

#18 Political Problem Solving

In a state and local government or social problems course, have students write a letter to their state senator or representative on the worst social problem. Have students explain why it is the worst problem. Then, have them state what should be done to solve the problem.

#19 Case Study: Examining a Social Problem

In the first week of a social problems course, have students write a paragraph describing an individual or a group with a social problem.

Have students analyze in another paragraph why the problem occurred, and what the cause might be.

Have students share their thoughts in small groups. Then process the thinking of the groups. Use the groups' thinking as the basis for introducing basic theories of social problems.

#20 Ethics across the Curriculum

In a given discipline, have students write a major paper that identifies a moral dilemma within the discipline and analyze the dimensions of that moral dilemma.

Approaches for exploring moral dilemmas include studying an issue or examining a case study of a particular situation.

Have students incorporate a number of variables when exploring the moral dilemmas:

◆ Establish the pertinent facts and information.

◆ Define the crux of the moral dilemma and the various perspectives stemming from the dilemma.

◆ Identify the moral options available to those with power.

◆ State the ethical principles relevant to this situation. Are some principles at odds with other principles?

◆ State the consequences relevant to this situation. Are some consequences more important?

◆ State what should be done and why. Explain why it is the best option on ethical grounds.

The topics on which this series of ethical analyses focus can vary a great deal, depending on the course. In courses on social problems or international economics, students can explore the moral dimensions of food aid to other countries and to the poor. In business courses, students can explore the moral dimensions of corporate responsibilities.

Again, case studies in these areas also work well. Do tobacco companies have an obligation to put themselves out of business? Should there be preferential hiring for minorities? Should the last hired be the first fired?

#21 Political Science: Setting Priorities

In a course on state and local government, have students write a two- to three-page policy memo on one of the following scenarios, and have them provide the reasoning behind their recommendation.

*   Examine the budget of a city. Expenditures are growing faster than revenues. To balance the budget, recommend a 10 percent cut to the budget.

*   State what you would cut. Why did you choose these areas for cuts over other areas? What impact do you project for the cuts?

*   Examine the budget of a city. Expenditures are growing faster than revenues. To balance the budget, recommend a 10 percent tax increase.

*   State what you would tax. Why did you choose those items to tax? Why these taxes instead of others? What impact do you project for these tax increases?

*   Before collecting these memos, have students discuss their reasoning with one another.

#22 Analyzing Political Writing

Give the following assignment to students:

1. Find and read an article concerning some political issues.

2. Obtain a copy of the article, or if possible the article itself, and turn it in with the assignment.

3. Write out the following information about the article:

    a) Does the article have a conclusion? If so, what is it?

    b) Do you agree or disagree with the conclusion? Why?

    c) List at least five questions you would like to ask the author concerning the article.

    d) Explain what kind of information you expect to receive from each of the questions raised in part (c).

#23 Family and Health

In a sociology course on family systems or on aging, present students with a problem-solving situation: Their sole surviving parent has become very ill from Alzheimer's disease. As the eldest child, the student is chiefly responsible for determining the parent's treatment.

Have students identify four or five criteria that represent the most important concerns in determining treatment. With those criteria in place, have them explore four situations as if they were placing the parent.

#24 Thinking about Anthropology

Students should imagine themselves at a dig in the "four corners" area where the borders of New Mexico, Colorado, Utah, and Arizona meet. They come across pottery of the Anasazi from the 13th century. This period immediately predates the disappearance of the Anasazi from the region.

Allow students to ask 10 questions to help them develop a theory about what happened to the Anasazi. The questions determine the information available for the theory.

What 10 questions will they ask?

#25 *Compare and Contrast*

In a cultural anthropology, comparative religion, or historic overview course, have students compare and contrast the basic structure of different societies. In this writing, have students assess the positive and negative aspects of different societies. For example, compare and contrast the highly industrial life in the United States with agrarian life in China and with hunting and gathering Aboriginal life in Australia.

In the process of writing, have students focus on how the structure of technology, the economy, and organizations affect people.

#26 *Psychology: Developing a Hypothesis*

Early in the 20th century, Sigmund Freud developed the theories that led to modern psychology.

Have students describe in detail one of Freud's theories. Then have them discuss new evidence that has implications for Freud's theory. How does the new evidence relate? Does it confirm, invalidate, or alter the theory?

If there is invalidation or alteration, what would the new theory based on the evidence be?

#27 *Questioning an Alien*

In an anthropology, history, sociology, or political science course, engage students in this writing exercise at the beginning of a course:

Have them imagine that they have come in contact with an alien being from another planet. Ask students to generate 10 specific questions to help them best understand life on the alien planet.

Process the lists in small groups and then with the whole class. What are the 10 best questions? Have each small group select five.

After processing those of the whole class and establishing a list of the 10 best, give the theory that underlies the best way to understand another culture.

#28 *Doing Historical Research*

Have students use their date of birth as a basis and go back 50 years. Have them choose a periodical published at that time, and have them find the chief issues discussed in the publication.

Have students then bring this research to class and put together a historical overview. In the process, identify emerging trends and discuss them.

#29 *Evaluating Primary-Source Evidence*

Provide students with primary-source material from which they are to make inferences and judgments about a culture or a historic time period. Evidence or material can vary from corn to music, from statistical data to other artifacts.

This activity can provide fine insights into the validity of inference and assumptions. For example, in a course focusing on the 1920s, show a film such as *The Jazz Singer*, listen to some music from Tin Pan Alley, and study census data. From these pieces of evidence, have students draw inferences about the culture.

#30 *Statistical Analysis*

Have students review sections of the latest census data from the federal government. After reviewing the data, have students submit one typewritten page with the following analytic steps:

◆ Develop a list of trends apparent from your review.

◆ Analyze what factors could explain the trends (be as creative as possible).

◆ Suggest how you could determine which factors would be the real causes for the trend.

#31 *Determining What Matters*

Have students write for two minutes in response to the question, What is true in this room now? After students have listed a number of facts, initiate a discussion about which details are significant and how we decide.

In a history course, explore some of the structures of organizing history. On a basic level use the concepts of setting, character, plot, action, and time to demonstrate selectivity.

#32 Observation and Inference

Another use of source material is rooted in first-hand observation. In an introductory sociology course, send students to a shopping mall. Have them observe and record the facts worth noting.

Based on the observation, have them create assumptions and draw inferences.

Have students bring their writings on the observations, the assumptions, and inferences, and share the information in small groups. Process the small-group results.

Collect the writing to verify the work.

Another variation of this process is to have students observe television (perhaps situation comedies) and draw inferences about the American family.

How do students determine what is worth noting?

#33 Encourage Note Taking

Today's students need encouragement on the value of taking notes and on how to take notes. One way to promote note taking is to formulate a couple of questions at the conclusion of treating important information: What is the one key idea of the past week? What don't you understand as well as you would like?

After writing responses to questions like these, have students exchange and review the notes of the other students. Ask students to generate questions to improve their understanding of the material. This activity can provide a good method of review for examinations.

Another variation on note taking is to gear the note taking to the reading. Have students identify the 10 key concepts (or historical characters or events) in the reading. Have students exchange lists to compare their answers.

#34 Listening for Writing

Have students listen to lectures or presentations without taking notes.

Following the lecture, have students write 150 words about the central idea in the lecture. Put students in groups to discuss the writing. Collect the writings and read a few aloud to the class.

#35 Reading Guide

Require students to respond in writing to these items about a reading assignment:

◆ Predict from the title what the reading assignment is about.

◆ Give a brief summary of the reading.

◆ List unfamiliar terms and define them.

◆ Answer a set of assigned questions.

This assignment helps focus students on what the author said.

#36 Nobel Prize in Literature

In a literature course, as part of the final or near the end of the term, have students select the writer most deserving of a Nobel Prize in Literature. Students should make their selection from among the authors they read during the term.

Students should use at least two types of criteria:

◆ What is the outstanding contribution of the author selected?

◆ Why is this author preferable to the others?

Have students compare and contrast the selection with two other writers.

#37 Writing about Viewing

In courses in which themes play a role, show a pertinent film. Have students analyze the film in writing from the perspective of the central ideas in the course. Use this writing as the basis for small-group and entire-class discussions.

For example, in an American history course looking at Vietnam, show a video on President Lyndon B. Johnson's dilemmas. Stop the tape and ask students to write what Johnson should have done and why.

#38 Writing Down Oral History—Community Experience

Using members of the community or places in the community can add a dimension to a student's understanding of history.

In oral history interviews, have the student start the interview with these types of statements: "It isn't here anymore," or "It used to be different." The subject should elaborate on "it" and how things changed. Is it better or worse? Why?

In looking at places, how has the place changed over time? How was it used? How have functions changed? Why? What was its origin? What is unique about its structure? What can it tell us about changes in the community?

#39 Linking Theory to Community Life

In a history course, have students visit a museum or an exhibit and link the experience of the visit to the theory of the course. For example, on a course examining the impacts of the Industrial Revolution, have students visit an art institute and view art of the time period.

Have students write a two-page report about three works of art to illustrate ideas and theories from the course. In their writing, have students address what, in particular, interested them in the art, and why they chose those three works of art. Finally, have students discuss what they learned from the experience.

#40 Analysis of Class Session Video/Audio

For students who miss class, one solution is to tape the class session on audiotape or videotape. To avoid penalties for absence, students need to view or listen to the tape and then write 150 words summarizing the central point of the class session.

#41 Daily Accountability Quizzes

In courses in which regular reading assignments are essential to the course's methodology, a problem may exist in getting students to do the reading. Daily accountability quizzes, with short essay questions, can solve this problem. Grading can be done simply by grading half or a third of the quizzes, enough to establish the accountability of the students.

#42 Essay Take-Home Final

To focus on student thinking, a final take-home essay could ask students to write "all they know" about a specific topic in a certain number of pages. A variation on this is to have students write reflective essays on what they have learned, either on a topic or in the course as a whole.

#43 In-Class Essay Test

To help students benefit from an in-class essay test, two twists might highlight the essay test itself. First, consider giving the essay questions to the students before the day of the test. Alternatively, instead of giving the essay questions early, allow students to bring a four-by-six-inch index card with crib information for the test.

#44 Practice Essay Exams

In the two weeks before midterm and final examinations, give students 20 to 25 minutes to write a practice or sample essay answer to a model examination question. The question should be based on recently completed course material.

Have the students meet in pairs and exchange exams. Ask them to read each other's exam and discuss strengths and weaknesses. Have one or two volunteers read a good answer. Then discuss the features of a good essay, possibly by distributing a model essay.

#45 *Writing for Efficiency*

In response to a reading, either fiction or nonfiction, give students an in-class assignment to write answers using a limited number of words to respond to 10 to 15 questions.

If students exceed the maximum number of words specified for each answer, deduct points. This penalty encourages students to avoid writing for writing's sake.

This assignment can be done by allowing students to use their own notes or not, as the faculty member prefers.

#46 *Linking Public Events to Personal Life*

In a course such as contemporary American history, have students write a three- to four-page paper linking their lives to public events. Have students read an essay such as Alice Walker's "The Civil Rights Movement: What Good Was It?" In this way students can span the gap between public and private life.

#47 *Journal Writing*

Have students write on key themes, such as freedom, authority, or change. They can do this in a journal and incorporate one to two pages of writing in response to reading an essay or excerpt of a larger work. Structured questions on the reading can ensure thoughtful reading and writing.

To help students structure a journal entry, create a series of questions for them to answer:

◆ Which one or two items were important?

◆ What surprised you?

◆ What should we review in class? Why?

◆ What can you apply to your own experience?

Depending on the course, journals may also be used to summarize problem solving in the discipline. For example, a journal in a mathematics class could be used to explain how difficult math problems are solved and conceptualized.

In any course students can communicate with the faculty member through the journal about any aspect of the course. Comments can range a great deal, from statements of frustration, praise, or bewilderment about the course to personally oriented responses.

#48 *Sequence Writing: Assessing One's Own Writing*

In a writing course or a writing-intensive course in one of the disciplines, have students write a series of papers:

◆ summary

◆ descriptive essay

◆ comparison/contrast essay

◆ persuasive essay

These four pieces of writing should be sequential and build on each other. They may vary according to the discipline and curriculum. Below are listed a series of questions based on each of the four papers. They are formulated to make students think about the act of writing itself. The questions provide an antidote to pigeonholing.

Summary Writing

1. What process did you follow when writing your summary? Describe the process.

2. If you had the essay to do over again, what would you change about the process? In other words, would you approach a second summary assignment differently? How?

3. What did you find most difficult about the assignment?

4. How did you overcome that difficulty?

5. What did you like about the assignment?

6. Can you think of any ways writing a summary has taught you about reading/studying/thinking? In other words, what skills have you acquired from the assignment that you might apply elsewhere? Describe.

Descriptive Essay

1. How did you approach this essay? What process did you use?

2. How was this essay different from the essay of summary? What ideas from writing the summary did you incorporate in this essay?

3. What did you like most about this essay? What were your strengths?

4. What did you like least? What were your weaknesses?

5. What problems (if any) did you have on your summary?

6. What have you done to solve those writing problems in this paper?

7. What have you learned about writing from this assignment?

Comparison/Contrast Essay

1. Where did you get your ideas for this essay?

2. Did you approach it differently than you did the description? Describe.

3. What did you like most about this essay? What were your strengths?

4. What did you like least? What were your weaknesses?

5. What problems have you had on previous papers? Have you solved them here? How?

6. What have you learned about writing from this assignment?

7. Can you think of ways you can use ideas from the comparison/contrast essay on other essays? Other school assignments? Your work?

Persuasive Essay

1. How would you rate your performance on this essay compared with the others you have written?

2. What were your strengths in writing this paper?

3. What were your weaknesses?

4. What have you learned about writing from this exercise?

5. How might you be able to put to use the strategies you have learned in writing the persuasive essay?

6. If there is one thing you know you need to continue to work on (even after this course is over), what is it?

7. How has your writing improved over the quarter?

8. What is the most valuable thing you have learned about writing this quarter?

#49 Sociology: Sequence of Short Writes

In an introductory course (or a more advanced course in criminal justice studies or social problems), have students assume the role of decision maker. They play the role of chief of police.

Racial tension is growing in inner-city neighborhoods. Following confrontations between police and teenagers, reports come in to the police chief's office of looting, vandalism, and violence. One group of advisers wants an aggressive show of force with weapons and mass arrests. The other wants to downplay the violence by sending police negotiators in to talk to local community leaders.

Which option does the student choose?

Have students write in one page why they chose that option and discuss it.

In the following class meeting, have students write a memo to the advisers whose advice they did not take. This one-page piece of writing should explore the reasoning, evidence, and assumptions for their dissent from that advice.

Have students discuss these memos in a small group. Process the small-group discussions with the whole class.

#50 *Probing through Writing*

Throughout the term give a series of assignments that explore a topic from a variety of perspectives. The topic may vary according to the course. For example, in a sociology course have students respond to questions about a specific culture, for example,

◆ Write about your knowledge of Chicano culture. How has it been formed? What historic influences are central in the culture's formation? What are some descriptive terms for Chicano culture?

◆ Interview three people outside of class and ask them a series of questions about Chicano culture. Summarize each interview in one page. Which interview was the most informative? Why?

◆ Make an annotated bibliography of eight to 10 articles and books on Chicano culture.

◆ Write a research paper of 10 pages on some aspect of Chicano culture. Compare and contrast Chicano culture with another culture.

#51 *Research and Writing*

In a course on social problems, technology, or communications, have students create a social research project on television and its social impact. The project should include the following steps:

◆ Review the literature on this topic in the library. Bring a list of the 10 articles and books that interest you most.

◆ Based on your reading of those articles, create your own research project. Bring a draft to class that describes the purpose of the research and how it will be done. Details should explore problems as well. These drafts will be discussed in small groups in class.

◆ Conduct a pilot study to gain some sense of the satisfactory nature of the research. In this pilot, observe the situation to determine the worth and the appropriateness of the factors in your research. Revise your research in writing. Discuss these revisions in small groups in class.

◆ Conduct the research project with the revisions incorporated. Write a report on your research that states the results and then analyzes those results with conclusions.

◆ Write a one-page summary for discussion with other students in a small group.

#52 *Developing a Personal Perspective*

After students have reached the midterm in any course involving multiple perspectives or multiple theories, use the following writing activity to help them develop a personal perspective.

Give the students a handout with two separate paragraphs containing contradictory viewpoints. Have students select the viewpoint with which they agree, and have them write why they chose it.

Next give students a descriptive piece of writing and ask them to interpret that piece through the viewpoints implicit in the initial two paragraphs. Again, have students follow this with a personal piece of writing that explains what their own view is.

Another variation on this process is to hand out two contradictory articles on any topic and have the students use the same approach.

#53 *Responding to a Text*

In a history class, distribute an excerpt from Karl Marx's *Communist Manifesto*. Have students read the excerpt for eight to 10 minutes. Then have them "free write" a stream-of-consciousness response to any aspect of the reading for three to four minutes. Put students in small groups for approximately 10 to 12 minutes to discuss what they wrote.

Following this, process the information stemming from the small groups. Then, have each student write two sentences that embody what the student believes and finds to be true from thinking about Marx. There is considerable latitude here, but the two sentences should draw on the reading, writing, and talking done earlier in the classroom session.

At this point (time permitting) have each student read the two sentences aloud without response or group comment. Collect the writing, and assemble a list of the two-sentence statements. Distribute that list to students in the next class meeting. Have students pick a two-sentence statement, either their own or that of another student, and develop that idea into a draft for a four- to six-page paper. Give students time in class to develop the idea in writing.

#54 *Using Television for Political Analysis*

Have students watch the local evening news on two different television channels, as well as the national evening news. Have them do the same with the late-night news. Tell students to read the local newspaper and the *New York Times* on the following morning. Have them answer the following:

Which items did they find were consistent at the various times and in the different media? Which items appeared in only one television setting? Which items in the newspaper were not on television?

Then have students develop theories to explain which items were on television and which were not. After students report the factual information in a couple of pages, have them write a two-page analysis on which type of items make the television news.

#55 *Social Problems and Critical Thinking*

Distribute an excerpt of writing with a distinct point of view concerning a social problem. Ask students to identify in writing (two pages) key definitions of the problem, evidence of the problem, key values, origins of the problem, its consequences, and possible solutions found in the excerpt. In each case, ask students to assess in writing (one page) how well the author did in clarity, depth, breadth, and consistency. Conclude this analysis with an overall assessment of the merits of the author's point of view (one page).

Have students share their thinking in small groups, and process in the large group.

#56 *History and Evidence*

At the beginning of a history class, ask students how we know about the past. How do we gather evidence? Have them each write for five to seven minutes on this question.

In small groups have the students share their thinking.

Following the small-group work, give students a couple of archaeological case studies that focus on the issue of evidence and conclusions. How do these case studies fit with the writings of the students?

Again, have students discuss the question in small groups. Process the results in the large class group.

#57 *The American War in Vietnam and Research: Historical Method*

After presenting students with a brief statement of facts about the duration of the war, fatality numbers, and costs, have students discuss why the war in Vietnam was fought.

Create teams of three or four students to discuss this issue. Have them create a strategy for how they would find better evidence to answer the question. Have them, as a group, gather the evidence.

Based on the evidence, have each member draft an explanation; bring these writings together, share them, and come out with a new team approach.

Have students share their approaches with the whole class.

#58 *Geography and Reasoning*
To combat the tendency in many geography courses to focus on facts, start the course with a five-minute write on the question, What is the relationship between human culture and geography?

After students conclude their writing, put them in small groups to discuss the question.

Process the answers in a large group. Use this as the occasion to introduce the three or four central concepts of the course.

#59 *Global Awareness*
In an environmental studies course, have students examine maps of the continents or a globe. After they have looked at the selected area, put them in small groups. Ask them to identify areas that are hostile to human habitation. Why are they hostile? If humans lived there, what alterations to the environment would be necessary for long-term human survival? How would those alterations affect plant, animal, and other life in the ecosystem?

After eight to 10 minutes of discussion in the teams, process the answers with the whole class.

#60 *Court Cases as Social Issues*
In a sociology, political science, ethics, or legal studies course, select a court case to use as the basis of analysis. Prominent, contemporary cases,

such as the Oklahoma or Waco bombing trials, are best. By choosing cases with volatility, the benefits of clear reasoning are exhibited more easily.

Students need to be provided with a one- to two-page summary of the incident giving rise to the court case, as well as a summary of the decision by the jury. With this information in hand, have the students work independently to answer the following questions:

- What is the central issue? How do the facts relate to this issue?

- What are possible, different interpretations of the issue? What evidence supports varying interpretations?

- Which evidence is most compelling? Why?

- What conclusion do you draw?

After students spend 10 minutes working independently by writing the answers to these questions, have them get in small groups to discuss their thinking. Ask the groups to reach consensus, like a jury, to the degree possible.

After eight to 10 minutes of small-group discussion, process the answers in the large group.

#61 *Persuasion and Advertising*
In a speech, mass communication, or mass culture course, explore the method used in print and video advertising to sell a product. Have students select three or four pieces of print advertising to bring to class. The faculty member could bring a videotape of commercials to illustrate the use of language and image.

Put the students in groups of three. First, have them examine their print advertisements. They should analyze the language and imagery for the inferences in the advertisement. What evidence is introduced to lead the reader to the conclusion?

Ask each group to share two of their examples with the whole class.

Following this, show the videotape. At the end of each commercial, ask for comments on inference, evidence, and conclusion.

While this method works fine for product advertising, it can also be used for political analysis of candidate advertising or issues advertising.

#62 History and National Character

In a course focusing on a specific nation or region, select a historic episode in which the representatives of the nation or region were judged to have acted poorly. For example, in a European history course, focus on the Nazi behavior in Germany. In an American history course, examine the McCarthy "Red scare."

To illustrate the issue, bring a one- to two-page excerpt describing the historic phenomenon and its moral violations.

At this point, ask the students if the contemporary population and culture of that nation or region is capable of the same behavior now. Have them write for four to five minutes on why or why not. Ask them to detail their thinking with specific assumptions, evidences, and conclusions.

Put students in small groups to discuss their writing. Then process the comments with the whole class.

#63 Technology and History

In a history course, have students identify the key technological innovations of a particular period and list them on the board. From that list of three to eight, have them choose which one is the most important.

Why are these the key innovations? Which is the most important for this historic period? Why?

Have them write for five to seven minutes on why that technological innovation was the most

important. What are the consequences of that technology? How were lives changed by it? Why are these changes more significant than those stemming from other technologies? Were there negative consequences from the technology? What?

After five to seven minutes of writing, have students critique each other's papers based on the adequacy of their answers.

Process the answers in the large group.

#64 Community Observation/Involvement

For a field experience course, send students to a community setting to observe and analyze. If there are principle forms of analysis, have students observe to confirm or refute the analysis.

In a course on individualism and community, require 20 hours of community service. Have students keep journals and write papers on their observation and analysis.

These pieces of writing can form the basis for discussion in traditional classroom settings, as well as in a weekend seminar.

#65 Critical Thinking: Social Problems/Applied Ethics

Take a case study for students to examine casually in the large group of a class. The case can be of an individual or institution reaching a decision. It should exemplify factors in the reasoning of that individual or institution. Use this case study in the large group to teach students a method of analysis. Have them identify the elements in the reasoning of the individual or institution. In this process of identification, ensure that at least five elements emerge:

◆ Definition: What is the definition of the issue or problem? What information informs the definition?

◆ Point of view: What is the perspective involved? What values inform this perspective?

◆ Conclusion/solution: What was the decision reached? What conclusion or solution stems from the reasoning?

◆ Evidence: What evidence is relevant to the conclusion/solution?

◆ Consequences: What consequences are caused by the decision? How does cause-and-effect function?

After identifying these five items, give students a one- to two-page case study on another topic. Have them write for 12 to 15 minutes on these areas:

◆ Summarize the author's reasoning using the five categories above.

◆ Using the five categories, critique the author's thinking for its adequacy or inadequacy.

In the large group, process responses as time permits.

#66 *Historical Research: Family Genealogy*

In the beginning of a history or literature course, ask students to conduct research on a member of their family to learn the elements in the member's personal story.

To give focus to the research, have students choose an aspect of their family member's life and relate it to history. For example, relate a great-grandparent's immigration to the United States to immigration trends.

Have students conduct research in two ways—written and oral. Oral research involves interviewing; at least one interview should be required. Written research can span anything from private journals and family clippings to public newspapers, magazines, and books.

At the completion of the assignment, have students discuss them in small groups before turning them in.

#67 *Focused Journal Writing*

In a course with primary-source materials (novels, poems, nonfiction works, but not textbooks), have students keep a journal with three entries per work. Each entry should be approximately 200 words.

Have students begin each entry by focusing on a key passage in the reading; this can be anything that engages the student. After copying the quotation, have students respond to the quotation.

The response could include these elements:

◆ amplification of what the author is saying

◆ relevance to student's life, or lives of others

◆ truth or falsity in statement

◆ other elements of student's choosing

At the conclusion of a longer work of fiction or nonfiction, include an additional summary and analysis entry. This final entry would include these items:

◆ author's perspective on the human condition and its disposition (hope–pessimism, good–evil)

◆ student's understanding gained from the book about human condition

Have students use their journal entries as the basis for small-group discussion in class. Process the small-group comments with the whole class.

#68 *Biography as Insight*

In any area of the college curriculum, faculty can identify pivotal individuals who were important in advancing knowledge in a given domain.

Provide students with a bibliography detailing the biographies of important figures within the purview of the course. Have students select one of those biographies and read it.

Require a five-page paper that illustrates the relationship of that individual's life and contributions to the particular field. Was any portion valuable personally to the student? Would the student recommend it to others?

Use these papers as the basis of discussion in small groups and with the whole class.

#69 *Learning Experiences beyond the Classroom*

In addition to traditional classroom activities, have students complete two relevant learning experiences beyond the classroom. These experiences could include the following:

◆ plays, performance art

◆ public readings by authors

◆ museums, galleries

◆ film, videotapes

◆ television

Ask students to elaborate in two to three pieces of writing on the relationship of these experiences to the course content. What did they learn? How valuable was the experience? Deficiencies? Would they do such an activity again of their own choosing?

#70 *Free Writing*

At the conclusion of a particular unit in any course, ask students to write all that they know about that information for eight to 10 minutes. They should do this without their notes. They should also keep writing as much as possible without regard for coherence or sequence.

#71 *Reading and Teaching: Psychology Summary*

In a psychology chapter of assigned reading (or any textbook in a course), there may be 12 to 15 sections in the chapter. At the start of class, assign a section to two or three students depending on class size.

Give the students five minutes to review the section with the other individual(s) assigned to that section. Then rotate the students every four to five minutes, so that each student gets to teach the section 11 to 14 times and to listen to different sections from other student-teachers.

#72 *Ethical Dilemma*

Ask students to write a short response and rationale to this ethical dilemma:

Imagine you are the president of the college and it is your responsibility to set tuition and the operating budget. You have three options:

◆ Keep tuition at present levels and limit enrollment.

◆ Serve more students by raising class size and faculty workload.

◆ Raise tuition to increase revenue and expand offerings.

Which option would you pick? Why?

After the short writing response, have students discuss their thinking in groups of two. Process a couple of responses with the whole class.

#73 *Writing a Major Paper*

In a course in which the student has a choice in developing a major paper, have students respond to the following items:

◆ title

◆ purpose, why selected

◆ major questions of interest

◆ sections of paper, classifications, categories

◆ how and when you will work

◆ what will be needed to do a quality job

◆ major concerns

Have students form groups of two to discuss their paper proposals.

#74 *Essay Test: Q & A*

In any course, ask students to develop three questions for the essay section of a midterm or final examination. The questions should explore the reasoned judgment of the students, not just a statement of fact or just a statement of personal taste.

With each of the three essay questions, have students provide model answers.

This assignment can be used in a number of ways. First, it can be counted as a regular assignment and graded. Second, it can be used in small groups to promote student learning. Finally, questions for the actual examination can be drawn from the student-generated questions.

#75 *Dramatic Interpretation of Theory*

In any course that compares the ideas of two theoreticians, have students construct a dramatic dialogue between the two.

Mandate that more than half of the dialogue contain direct quotations of the theoreticians from their works.

Read the best two to the class.

Keep in mind that the authors or theoreticians do not have to be contemporaries. The dialogue can take place across time and place.

#76 *Three-Word Characterization*

In any sociopolitical course in which concrete examples are used, consider the use of the three-word characterization to promote student reading and thinking about the reading.

After reading the case study/concrete example, have students choose three separate words to characterize the reading.

Use this three-word characterization as the basis for small-group discussion and the subsequent entire class process.

#77 *Political-Economic Systems*

In a theory course in political science or economics, after finishing an overview contrasting capitalism and socialism (or democracy and communism), create a list of characteristics attributable to either system.

Have students determine which characteristics fit which system. Put students in pairs to see if any confusion exists. After they compare notes, take questions to clarify.

#78 *Assessing Prior Learning in a Political Science Course*

In the beginning of a course on state and local government, construct a series of 10 statements that are a mixture of truth and falsehood. Ask students to respond on a five-point scale (1–Definitely true, 2–Probably true, 3–Don't know, 4–Probably false, 5–Definitely false).

Collect the anonymous responses to determine the knowledge level.

#79 *Sociological Analysis*

In an introductory sociology course (or a history course), have students analyze in writing what is involved in sociological data. While data certainly are factual, typically assumptions are built into the data. For example, in analyzing unemployment statistics, there is the question of the definition.

This analysis would distinguish reasoned judgment from fact. Have students discuss the analysis with each other.

#80 *Writing in Midstream*

In any given course, especially one documented by lecturing, stop in the middle of the class. Ask students to write down questions they have. What remains unclear?

Collect the questions and answer them.

#81 Sex, Marriage, and Family: Assessing Options

In a sociology course on sex, marriage, and family, ask students to assess whether or not they would consider living together as an option to marriage. Have students draw a list of pros and cons individually.

Then have them discuss their thinking in small groups to see if the groups can achieve consensus.

#82 Thinking through Conflict

In any class with controversy, the exchange of opinions sometimes becomes heated. Diffuse the atmosphere through writing.

Have students summarize the point of view of person #1 and of person #2 in two or three sentences for each. Then have them conclude with three sentences on their own point of view.

Use this writing as the basis for small-group discussion.

#83 Geography and Urbanization

In a geography course, have students examine a map of South America and identify the four largest cities. Have the students analyze why those cities are the largest.

#84 Social Structure and War

Have students gather empirical data on World War II. Collate that data into categories such as the following:

◆ Material interests
◆ Political interests
    Ideology
    Geopolitical concepts

◆ Psychological concerns
    Honor, credibility
    Coercive diplomacy
◆ Military arsenals

Based on the data organized into these categories, ask students to formulate a theory that uses each category and its data to explain how that reality played a role in causing World War II.

#85 Biology and Demographics

Have students write one page in class on the relationship of human population growth to food, food production, and birth and death rates.

Then give students a short summary of the Club of Rome's Limits to Growth (1972). Do students agree or not? Why?

Have students write a one-page response to the summary.

#86 Gerontology

In a sociology or human services course dealing with gerontology, put the students in the position of policymaker. Have them analyze the current state of affairs by studying social security, health care, and nursing homes. Ask them to write a two-page letter to the governor with at least four concrete suggestions for improving conditions for the elderly.

CHAPTER FOUR

Spoken Thought: Collaborative, Cooperative Learning and Socratic Exchanges

Students develop their thinking not only through writing but also through speaking. A variety of options exists for faculty to use when engaging students verbally. One method of classifying these options is to categorize in terms of the audience; that is:

◆ student-to-student speech (collaborative or cooperative learning)

◆ student-faculty speech (Socratic exchanges)

The most dominant type of speech pattern, that of a faculty member lecturing, has been omitted. The only way faculty will know whether students have been engaged in active listening is to have them write or speak about what they heard.

Collaborative learning (student-to-student speech) has several forms depending on the faculty member's specific goals. Collaborative learning has some generic characteristics regardless of the spe-

cific goals. Faculty place students in groups and give them an assignment, or activity, to complete. All groups have two objectives—a collaborative interaction objective, and an academic, subject-matter objective. The collaborative interaction objective involves group process and group dynamics. Students use and develop small-group, interpersonal skills. By talking face-to-face, students learn to function in teams and to work interdependently.

Collaborative learning attempts to alter the classroom and its dynamics by engaging students in learning with their peers and in cooperative efforts with faculty. The active, responsible orientation of speaking and thinking in the group makes collaborative learning a powerful tool.

Collaborative, cooperative learning may vary from peer teaching to learning communities. The common thread, however, stems from thinking in a community of knowledgeable peers. In the process the student becomes a more active participant and assumes partial responsibility for the thinking of a community of thinkers.

Faculty hope to achieve several positive outcomes through cooperative, collaborative learning: Students will broaden their horizons by exposure to the thinking of others. Seeing themselves as thinkers is another possible positive result. Finally, groups can provide students with a sense of community and break through the anonymity of college. This can have a positive impact on learning retention.

A key variable in distinguishing the form of collaborative or cooperative learning is whether the activity is graded or not. If it is ungraded, the faculty member will usually set the task, dictate the size of the group, state the purpose, and give the time limitations. The positive outcomes listed above can be achieved under these conditions. If the activity is graded, faculty create more structure. They dictate group members, observe the in-class groups in discussion, and hold the individual members of the group accountable through testing and by assessing individuals as they explain group answers. Individuals can be selected randomly.

Research has revealed a number of findings about successful group design and grading. These findings include the following characteristics (Goodsell, et al. 1992):

♦ allocate 20 percent or more of the grade for group activity

♦ limit group presentations to one presentation per group

♦ provide classroom time for work on group assignments and giving one to three assignments

♦ consider group examinations

♦ include peer evaluation in the grade

♦ create ongoing groups of four or five students

Studies indicate that collaborative, cooperative learning can achieve better results than traditional lectures in terms of student comprehension, thinking skills, and motivation. It also can result in worse outcomes. Much is contingent on how adept the faculty member is in designing the collaborative, cooperative projects. Purpose, activity, and structure need to be clearly stated.

In the second broad classification of speaking as an active-learning strategy, student-faculty speech is designed to develop student thinking. This exchange is commonly identified as the Socratic exchange or Socratic dialog. In this form of speech, students respond to questions that faculty pose to them. This technique can work at its best in smaller, seminar-style courses. The technique is designed to assess the student's mastery of the subject matter and critical thinking in that context. The only parameters of this method are the time available and the range of questions pursued.

In faculty speech, the teacher should attempt to ask good questions and to exemplify good thinking. The exemplification, or modeling, of good thinking occurs when the teacher thinks aloud in front of the students. This process, in addition to embodying well-reasoned thought, is best when it displays a communicative, clear accessibility. When teachers speak in this fashion, they illustrate good thinking.

Finally, there are two other types of speaking as active-learning strategies that fall outside student-to-student and student-faculty speech. One is the presentation, or talk, by the individual student on a given topic. The other is the debate between two parties on a given topic.

Whatever the variety of speaking, the goal is to allow students to find their own "voice" and to develop their thinking in the process. While speech courses or personal development courses may have other goals, most faculty in a college or university could use student speaking to engage and assess student thinking.

SPOKEN THOUGHT: COLLABORATIVE, COOPERATIVE LEARNING AND SOCRATIC EXCHANGES

#87 *Cooperative Learning*

In courses that rely on primary-source material (or that could benefit from its inclusion), one method to use is that of cooperative learning. In teaching from textual material, especially with historic works, assign readings to students before the class meeting.

In the class period, create groups of three students. Give each student responsibility for a separate reading.

Student A	Reading 1
Student B	Reading 2
Student C	Reading 3

In the initial meeting of ABC, have the group discuss each reading, with the student assigned to the reading taking the lead. Allow 10 to 15 minutes for this preliminary meeting.

Then create groups of two students from those assigned a particular reading.

A B C	A B C		A B C	A B C	
AA	BB	CC	AA	BB	CC

Allow 10 minutes for discussion in these diads. An assignment may help to focus the discussion. For example, ask students to define the author's central point. Why was this controversial? Do you disagree with the author? Why?

For a third group, create new groups of ABC. Give each group 15 minutes, with each individual leading the discussion for five minutes on the assigned reading. In this time, the group should try to identify two questions per reading. After this 15-minute period, have the small groups return to the whole class.

For the final 10 to 15 minutes of class, process the questions of all the As, Bs, and Cs. These questions may well carry over into the following class.

This method can shift the responsibility for learning onto the students and make them active learners.

#88 *Small-Group Discussions*

Small groups of three or four students can be used to draw out the individual responses from students. Often engaging the students in a short writing response first will help them use the small-group setting more effectively.

Two examples of small-group exercises are problem-solving situations and case studies. After giving a written or verbal problem or case study, have students write a brief response and then discuss it. There are growing numbers of videotapes in which a problem or case study is given. These scenarios can be shown and then stopped after the description ends. Following the writing and small-group discussion, more of the tape's analysis can be used. An example of this is the use of the video *Ethics in America* in an ethics course.

Another approach to initiating students into the process of critical thinking is to use film. One example would be to use the film *Twelve Angry Men*, starring Henry Fonda. Have students watch the initial part of the film, to the beginning of the jury-deliberation process, and then ask the students to draw conclusions. The remainder of the film is a fine example of false assumptions and erroneous conclusions.

#89 Collaborative Definition

Form small groups of three or four students and have them introduce themselves to each other. Use the Declaration of Independence as the focus for discussion.

Have one person serve as a recorder while another reads a sentence aloud.

"We hold these truths to be self-evident, that all men are created equal, that they are endowed by their Creator with certain unalienable Rights, that among these are Life, Liberty, and the pursuit of Happiness."

Several terms are central in this passage:

◆ truths

◆ self-evident

◆ men

◆ created equal

◆ creator

◆ unalienable rights

◆ life

◆ liberty

◆ pursuit of happiness

Have the small groups define these items. Have the students rewrite the sentence so that it is stated using their terms and clarifies any confusion.

Allow the groups to then share their redefinitions and rewritten passages.

#90 Collaborative Decision Making

In social problems courses, students often become adept at stating several dimensions in the reality of problems facing society. One pitfall of this approach is that students can become paralyzed by the problems without gaining any vision of how to solve them.

To counteract this phenomenon, put students in groups of five. Give details of the same social problem to two groups. For example, a class of 30 students would break into six groups of five. The class would analyze three social problems, two groups per problem.

Have each group engage in a role-play in which the members function as a policymaking, legislative group with power. Each group should generate three specific laws to improve the social situation.

Each group needs to reach a consensus on the three laws.

Then have the groups report on their three pieces of legislation. Have the two groups considering the same social problem report consecutively, to compare and contrast their findings.

#91 Observation and Analysis

Have students observe five conversations between five different sets of two people. Assign different sets so that students observe mixtures of the following:

◆ man and woman

◆ young and old

◆ white and nonwhite

In observing, tell students to make note of the following elements:

◆ who talks more

◆ who interrupts whom

What do conversational quantity and interruption tell us about the relationships based on age, gender, or race? Is age, gender, or race the key variable that might explain the analysis? What is?

Students should write descriptive observations and analysis on the five conversations. Have students bring their writing to class to share in small groups. Then process the outcomes of their discussions.

#92 Q & A: Random Draw

As an incentive for students to complete assigned readings, tell them before class that you will randomly draw the names of eight to 10 students to answer eight to 10 key questions. The random nature of the questions should create an atmosphere in which students anticipate selection to answer the question.

If desired, points can be given for how satisfactory the answer is.

The best method of formulating the questions is to make them parallel the eight to 10 key points of the reading/lecture.

#93 Group Test Challenge

Give students an objective, multiple-choice test. Intentionally design the test so more than one answer per item is correct. Score the test, however, as if only one answer is correct per item. Have students take the test individually.

Return the corrected tests and put students into groups of four or five. Have students discuss the items that anyone in the group missed. Teams may submit written appeals, stating the rationale for the particular item appealed.

Respond orally to the successfully appealed items. This exercise is especially useful when demonstrating the complexity of any given item.

#94 Group Test, Peer Evaluation

For some portion of grading students, use a combination of group testing and peer evaluation.

Using groups of three to five students, give objective/short essay exams based on the lecture and the readings. Group testing allows students to discuss various aspects of each answer. You may find even the less talented and motivated students learning in this arrangement.

Combine this group-test situation with peer evaluation. In the peer evaluation, have members of the group assess the contribution of all those in the group to the group test. Create two or three questions with a forced-point distribution to members of the group for the peer evaluation.

#95 Peer Learning Groups

Early in the term create "peer learning groups" to provide mutual support during the course. Try to put students of varying knowledge and skill abilities into the groups of four or five. If possible, have at least one knowledgeable, organized person in each group.

The groups provide support for writing assignments and for test review. Make the last 15 minutes of class available on a periodic basis for these activities.

If students desire, they may use these groups outside of class meetings as study groups.

#96 Pro–Con Groups

Groups can be used to examine controversial ideas. Two groups can take opposing viewpoints and argue the pros and cons before the rest of the class. The pros and cons may be presented to two or three other members of the class who cross-examine those advocating a particular viewpoint. The rest of the class evaluates the persuasiveness of the two points of view.

In a course on Vietnam, for example, students might role-play two groups coming before Harry Truman and two advisers in 1950. One is a delegation of French diplomats who want to maintain control in Vietnam. The other delegation represents Ho Chi Minh and those wanting France out of Vietnam. The class evaluates the persuasiveness of the arguments.

#97 Social Problems: Debate

In the early stages of a course in social problems, develop a list of controversial topics that will be treated over the term. A sample list might include the following items:

- tuition-free higher education
- public housing
- universal health-care access
- capital punishment
- mandatory public service for young adults
- tax rate increases for the wealthy, corporations
- mandatory AIDS education in junior high, high school
- censorship

Put students in groups of four and have each group form two teams. Have each team develop arguments and evidence to support their position. Have each group briefly write the two major arguments in support of their positions.

Have each team discuss its arguments with the other side and take notes on the other side's perspective.

Students should keep their notes and present their arguments to the entire class at some time before the topic receives formal treatment in class.

After both sides present their arguments, have each person write 500 words on what they think and why, and submit this essay and notes.

#98 One-Person Presentations/Role-Plays

Panel presentations can often be used, but responsibility and quality of the presentation are often difficult to monitor. An option to the panel presentation is the one-person presentation. In history class, in particular, presentations on key individuals, movements, or ideas work well. With one student taking responsibility for a five- to seven-minute presentation, the quality is clearly in the students' domain. Depending on faculty preference, these presentations can be graded or ungraded.

Another way to structure the one-person presentation is to include a detailed question and answer format in which the class asks for follow-up information. In the case of presentations on historic personalities, this could allow for a full-blown role-play of that individual by the student. Questions could be taken on the order of *Meet the Press*.

Finally, in an attempt to build some link to the world beyond the classroom, have students attend a play, exhibit, performance, or film that is pertinent to the course, and use this as the basis of the presentation. Have students write a short paper as well.

#99 Role-Play and Processing

In courses ranging from social problems to ethics or public policy, put students in pairs. Have one student role-play a middle-aged male who is homeless and temporarily staying at a shelter. Have the other student role-play a social worker trying to help the homeless man.

Any role-play's value lies in the processing and analysis of the role-play. Analysis involves the following items:

- Did the roles meet the participants' expectations? How?
- What other dimensions would have added to the understanding?
- What generalizations about individuals and society can be made?

Students should explore these questions with another pair following the role-play.

#100 Feedback Loop

Ask students directly: What helps you learn? What can a faculty member do to help you learn?

Have students discuss these questions in small groups. Process the responses with the whole class.

Strive to implement their suggestions.

#101 *Interview the Professor*
At a point in the course before the midterm, have students interview the faculty member. Use the format of a press conference.

Have students ask why the course should be studied, what issues are significant and whatever else they think of.

This activity can be used to prepare for the test.

#102 *Student-Faculty Learning Conference*
During the final two to three weeks of the quarter, have students sign up for 15-minute meetings during faculty office hours. Before this conversation, have students write one to two pages responding to the following questions:

◆ What have I learned?

◆ What pleased me? Displeased me?

◆ How has my learning improved?

◆ What areas need improvement in my learning?

◆ What now?

These answers should be handed in before the conference for reference in the discussion.

#103 *Collaborative Learning: Division of Labor*
In a graded collaborative learning activity, it is important for the members of the group to have accountability for specific learning activities. One way to do this is to have the group systematically divide the labor among its members. For example, depending on the assignment, members might divide research, drafting, and editing tasks. This division of labor can be completed in class and submitted on a single sheet of paper.

#104 *The Other Point of View*
Choose two controversial topics for a pro–con argument in class. Have students choose a topic to engage. Then have individuals choose a position, pro or con, to advocate.

At that point, give them the other point of view to advocate; that is, if they choose pro, give them con, and vice versa.

Have them develop the arguments and select a spokesperson for the group. Have each side present its point of view.

Process how it was for students to argue from a different perspective and whether the exercise has changed their thinking.

#105 *Critical Reading and Collaboration*
At the start of class, give students a pertinent two- to three-page handout. Ask them to read it and identify its four key concepts.

Before doing this, it is beneficial to model critical reading: Use an editorial in the morning paper to illustrate the reasoning and inquiry process, for example.

After students have read the assignment privately, have them discuss it in small groups. Make sure they take notes and share how they came to identify the key concepts.

#106 *Beliefs*
Have students identify a belief they hold and why they have it. Have them do this in a three- to four-minute piece of writing.

Then have them state a contradictory belief and explain why individuals hold that belief.

#107 *Observation: Attributing Assumptions*
In any thoughtful person the skills of observation and objective recording are important, as is the ability to attribute assumptions.

To develop observation skills, provide students with photographs or excerpts of a videotape. Ask students to do two things:

◆ record what they see without interpretation

◆ provide interpretative assumptions to explain the video or photos

Have students respond in writing and then share their observations and assumptions with one another in small groups.

Another variation on this exercise is for the faculty member to tell a story that leaves much open to interpretation. Have the students provide assumptions to interpret.

#108 Research and Oral Reports

In any course, in the process of assigning papers, ask students to form two- or three-person panels on various topics. In conjunction with these panels, students must include two outside research sources for their comments.

Students should briefly attempt to clarify their positions and then write about them for three to four minutes.

Next, have students discuss their thinking in groups of three. Have two of the group ask questions and seek to understand the assumptions made by the writer.

#109 Multicultural Speeches

In any course attempting to infuse multiculturalism into the curriculum, have students give informative speeches on ritual, belief, values, and community from their own, or another's, perspective. The perspective should touch on ethnicity, race, gender, or religion.

#110 Panel Discussion

In a history course, assign students research tasks to develop their skills as historians. As one exercise, assign groups of three or four students to research cultural aspects of the local community. These aspects could touch on ethnicity, religion, race, economics, technology, or geography.

Ask students to keep a journal or write a short paper on their assigned area. In this writing, they should be conscious of writing as a historian.

At an appropriate point, have students share their insights from their writings by giving a panel presentation. Have students hand in their writing following the panel.

#111 Random Groups

One problem in using small-group collaboration is in developing new relationships among students in the course. It is important to remove anonymity from any learning community. To do this, use a random method to arrange the small groups. One method is to have students count off in groups of four in random ways. Another is to make up a grid by assigning a number to each student and putting the students into groups according to number.

This has the advantage of creating relationships among all students.

#112 Expert in the Field

In any course requiring one-person presentations, have students frame the presentation in a slightly different fashion. Challenge them to become "experts in the field." Have them identify a topic from a list in which they want to become proficient. Have them conduct library research as well as interviews where appropriate.

Encourage students to make the presentation as interesting as possible. In addition to promoting enthusiasm, have students tell why they chose the topic; the literature and interviews they used; and their analysis of these media, videos, simulations, and small-group involvement.

Challenge students to create three or four test items from their talks. Have them hand these items in at the completion of the talk.

#113 Small-Group Discussion of Summary Papers

After returning summary papers to students, have the students discuss the papers with one another in small groups. This activity is best done early in the term. Summarizing is such a building-block intellectual skill, and so geared to a common interpretation, that students can do well with it. Areas of consensus build confidence. Disagreement can be used to focus on the text and promote intellectual inquiry.

#114 *Group Problem Solving*

At the start of a class session for which reading was assigned, create groups of three or four students. Give them a problem to solve that is linked to their understanding of the reading.

At the conclusion of the problem-solving time, give students a method for determining the reporter in their groups. This can vary from earliest birth date in a calendar year to youngest in a family to those with a size eight shoe or closest. This method keeps all engaged as potential reporters.

#115 *Small Groups: Evaluating Performance*

In some courses it may be desirable to use small groups as a portion of the grading system for the course. In these settings it is essential to get student input. Here is a list of items to ask from the individuals in the group:

- How well did your group function? Excellent –Well–Satisfactorily–Poorly

- Give an example of something you learned from the group.

- Give an example of something the group learned from you.

- What grade would you give yourself?

- What grade would you give the other group members?

- How would you change the small group arrangement to improve it?

Before asking the group's members to complete this form, you may ask them to discuss their answers.

#116 *Group Readers*

To reinforce the importance of critical reading, create groups of three students. Assign each group of three responsibility for leading a discussion or making a presentation on the reading.

You may wish to prescribe a particular scheme for making a presentation. One method would be to have students write particular one-sentence or one-phrase responses to particular, specified pieces of reading. This method would ground the discussion in the reading itself.

If desired, part of the student grade could hinge on how well the presentation-discussion went.

#117 *Group Papers*

In a social problems course, create groups of four or five students. Every other week ask them to bring a copy of a social problem from the newspaper. They should also bring three or four copies so that each group member has one. While these should be on social problems, ensure that at least a couple of times, the articles treat a social solution.

Have the group briefly read the articles brought by the other members. They should then agree on one article for group analysis.

Give the group a form of analysis to use on the social problem–social solution. This analysis should involve elements of the thinking process— definition, assumptions, conclusions, evidence, logical consistency, and alternate points of view.

Each member should write four or five paragraphs of analysis. The group members should read one another's papers and select the best. Then they should revise that paper, if needed, and submit it as the group's paper.

Depending on how sophisticated a system you want to use, you could require each member of the group to contribute one paper. If the group does not elect to use a member's work, that person can submit an alternate assignment.

#118 *Class Discussion: Speaking and Listening*
In class discussion, promote critical speaking and listening by incorporating the adequacy of student response to question and answer. Assess this with a full–half–no credit grade.

Require that all students participate (either through a random method or by calling on students).

You should enable students to expand on the original question by asking them to elaborate, give an example, or relate the question to their own experience.

At any point, other students can be asked to paraphrase what the responding student said. They can then be asked if they agree or disagree and why.

The Critical Thinking Process: Writing and Speaking to Make Thinking Explicit Across the Curriculum

Regardless of the particular discipline in the college curriculum, knowledge exists that rests on information, assumptions, evidence, and reasoned conclusions. College faculty hope to engage students in this knowledge. By questioning, examining, and sifting through this knowledge they hope to assist students in becoming reflective thinkers. By focusing students on the elements of reasoning (point of view, assumptions, purpose, conclusion, consequence, inferences, problems, etc.), they begin to develop the habits of mind of critical thinking. They develop independence, courage, truthfulness, fair-mindedness, discipline, and civility, among other habits.

Faculty need to clarify the structure of thought as much as possible in their courses. Initially, this involves a generic look at thinking and thinking well. By focusing on models of critical thinking like those mentioned in chapter one, faculty reaffirm the common goal uniting teacher and student. They draw attention to the purpose of an education.

Faculty need to link the thinking in the course to the value of thinking in life. People adept at critical thinking are capable of actively gathering, conceptualizing, and using information as a guide to belief and action. They are capable of identifying misconceptions and deceit, as well as narrow-mindedness or bias. Critical thinkers use this thinking process in their personal and professional lives, for work and leisure, to attain the fullness of their humanity.

In addition to employing a generic look at critical thinking and the skills of thinking well, faculty need to focus explicitly on what it means to think well in their particular academic discipline and in that particular course.

Faculty need to make their implicit, private beliefs and thoughts as explicit and as public as possible. They should put in writing, as well as in visual depictions, what they think it means to think well in that course and discipline. While individual faculty may differ on particular areas, they need to set a course's context by identifying the central issues, questions, and assumptions.

Students need to be shown why the perspective of that course and discipline are important. The usefulness of the discipline should be manifest. Faculty can structure examples of problem solving or appreciation to illustrate this.

A key manifestation of knowledge acquisition and intellectual skills development is the movement of the student beyond the boundaries of egocentrism to a broadened perceptual framework. By focusing on the basic disciplinary framework of terms, key concepts, basic issues, and methodologies, students can evolve in their thinking to more complex operations. These operations include identifying and analyzing assumptions, comparing and contrasting ideas, creating a point of view, and evaluating arguments.

To do this in a particular course and discipline, faculty need all the teaching ability and talent they can muster. They must remove confusion from the thought in the discipline to the best of their ability. Sharing their point of view on the key thinking elements of a discipline and its course framework is a great starting point.

#119 Critical Thinking: A Diagnosis

Have students describe in writing a setting or circumstance in which they experienced or observed unfairness. In the writing they should also describe the response of the one treated unfairly and why that person was treated unfairly. Finally, the writing should evaluate the unfairness and why it was wrong.

This short piece of writing can be used as the basis for reasoning and critical thinking. By using the example of unfairness, students have a case study of poor reasoning. They can then examine the lack of sound reasons and sound assumptions in drawing questionable conclusions.

From this starting point, students can be shown the components of critical thinking:

- definition
- reasons
- assumptions
- conclusion

After reviewing these elements, students can diagnose pieces of writing by identifying those four features.

As students become more adept at diagnosing the elements of thinking, they can be taught some of the standard fallacies of reasoning. These should include the following abbreviated list:

- false cause
- emotional appeal
- non sequitur
- personal attack
- argument from authority
- either/or
- hasty conclusion
- false generalization

Students may be given pieces of writing or view speeches that contain these components, to assess the strength of the author's thinking.

In the evolution of student thinking, the next phase should move students to formulate counter-arguments on any given point of view. The students can also state their own position, and assess the soundness of each other's thinking.

#120 Structure of Thought

In a given course or part of a course, have students interpret a piece of thinking by focusing on the structure of thought.

One broad example of this is to focus on a theory in any given discipline and on how it relates to previous, existent theories. The development of new paradigms, as described by Thomas S. Kuhn in his *Structure of Scientific Revolutions* (1970) is an illustration of this process.

Have students describe the evolution of the new theory. Why did it surface? How did it come into existence? What new assumptions did the thinker bring into being? What is the new theory? What evidence was there for the new theory? How did it differ from earlier theories? How was it similar to earlier theories? What are the strengths of the new theory? What are the weaknesses of the new theory? What impact did the new theory have?

#121 Series of Questions in Response to Reading

Assign students readings by prominent writers and thinkers in a discipline, culture, or time period, and have them write responses to the following questions, to focus their thinking:

- What is the major insight of the thinker?
- Why do we remember this person?
- What assumptions are central in this thinking process?

- Are these insights still valid today?
- How are they applied today?
- What comments would this thinker make if alive today?

#122 Writing to Solve a Problem

Have students identify a problem. In a course with a historical or social orientation, this approach can succeed in crossing narrow disciplinary lines to create a holistic view of human problems. After students choose a problem, have them write brief responses to the following seven questions:

- What evidence exists that there was a problem?
- How was the problem defined?
- What alternatives existed?
- What were the pros and cons of each alternative?
- Which was the best alternative?
- Which alternative was actually chosen?
- What was the result of that choice?

After students write responses to these seven questions, they can discuss the answers in small groups. When they conclude the small-group discussion, process the responses in the large group. By embellishing the responses, the equivalent of a lecture can occur.

Finally, the merits of this problem-solving methodology for personal problems could also be mentioned.

#123 A Concept Map for Critical Thinking

Concept mapping provides a visual image, diagram, or map of our understanding (or lack of it) on a given topic. Concept maps include a number of concepts and the relationships of those concepts. The relatedness of concepts helps students to determine dominant ideas and subordinate ones, as well as to distinguish the general concept from a specific one.

Among the variety of purposes for concept mapping, it can be used in critical thinking to depict visually the structure of thinking.

Students can take the structure of critical thinking depicted in Figure 5.1 and play into it any examples of thinking in order to assess them.

#124 *Point of View*
Give students two or three differing points of view in the form of short essays and ask them to com-

pare, contrast, and evaluate the differing points of view.

Ask students first to summarize the arguments of each writer by commenting on the central argument and its supporting pieces of evidence leading to the writer's conclusion.

After summarizing, have the students find the similarities and differences in the short essays. In this process, the students need to pay attention to detail. Are the facts the same? Are differing

Figure 5.1 Concept Map: Critical Thinking

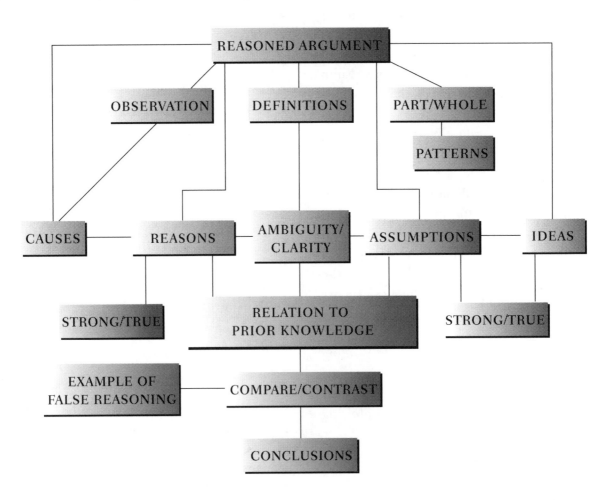

assumptions brought to the facts? What evidence is central in their thinking? What has led each writer to a certain conclusion?

Which conclusion is most compelling to the student? Why? What is the student's own conclusion?

In the social sciences or in ethics there are many anthologies that provide contrasting essays on the same topic. These would serve well for this assignment.

Another variant of this assignment is to use multiple perspectives on the same event and have students analyze them. Reports on the Democratic Convention in Chicago in 1968, the Tiananmen Square events in China in 1989, or the assassination of Archbishop Romero in El Salvador are all examples of this variant.

#125 *Assertive Essay/Challenge Essay*

Have students write a two-page essay in which they assert what they believe about a topic and why. Provide them with a choice, either of their own creation or from a list. They should rest their conclusions on evidence and assumptions that they believe to be defensible.

After students complete the writing, have them read their essays to each other in small groups. Permit discussion in the small groups.

Following the reading-discussion, have them write another two-page essay challenging the conclusions, evidence, and assumptions in the first essay. Again, have them read and discuss these counteressays.

#126 *Self-Assessed Thinking*

At the end of the course, have students assess their own thinking. This can be done as the faculty member chooses—either in the final or separately, as part of the grade or not, either anonymously or not.

Here is a list of basic questions to focus the students' self-assessment:

- How has my thinking improved in this course?

- What assignment and/or feedback most helped my thinking?

- What hindered my thinking most in this course?

- Based on this course, how would I assess my thinking strengths?

- Based on this course, how would I assess my thinking weaknesses?

- How will I improve upon my weaknesses? Which skills need improvement?

#127 *Peer Evaluation of the Thinking in an Essay*

Have students use the following five elements to evaluate thinking in each other's papers.

Points

- The central argument is clearly stated. (10 points)

- The assumptions, logic, and definitions are well-reasoned. (10 points)

- The conclusion follows and is backed up by the evidence. (10 points)

- The strongest point of the essay is _____. (10 points)

- The weakest point of the essay is _____. (if none, 10 points)

_____

Total Points (50 maximum)

#128 *Writing for Fact and Meaning*

Use either a reading or a video shown in class. Ask students to write responses to a series of questions in class. Have the initial question or two ask for factual information. Shift the remaining questions to analysis and evaluation.

For example, in a course on 20th-century American history, show a videotape on Prohibition. Ask students the following initial questions:

- What was the Volstead Act?

- Why did Prohibition become the law?

Shift the final questions to:

- What was right about Prohibition?

- What was wrong about Prohibition?

- Should drugs be legalized, like alcohol? Why or why not?

#129 Distinguishing Mental Activities

Discuss and analyze with students the differences among the following statements and mental activities:

- statements of fact

- inferences

- assumptions

- evidence

Give students a written text in an appropriate discipline. Have them classify each statement in the text according to these four categories.

Another option is to give students a videotape and ask them to do the same exercise. Political speeches are often a fertile ground for analysis.

#130 Question Asking

In an essay test, ask students to write the five best questions to indicate a thorough knowledge of the material.

To focus students on the critical thinking process in the course, have them identify the level of questioning using a tool such as Bloom's *Taxonomy* (1956).

#131 Designing a Final Test

Have students bring all the information in their notes and books to design the final test. In preparing the final test, instruct students to seek different kinds of knowledge. Factual knowledge and information can be ascertained through short essays or in true–false or multiple-choice questions. Another type of knowledge can be determined by analytical essay tests. Finally, have students construct evaluative, imaginative questions that ask for comparison and contrast.

#132 Critical Reading

Have students answer in writing a series of questions in response to a reading. The questions should engage the students directly in interpreting the reading. Questions should range from those seeking information and identification to those asking for analysis of the logic in thinking and for understanding points of view. In addition, students should be asked to evaluate the value of ideas in the reading and to compare and contrast them with their own.

#133 Modeling Critical Reading

Before making an assignment on note taking, model that behavior by showing students how you would read a selection.

For example, if you are asking students to identify the three major assumptions of the author in the reading, show students how you would complete the assignment.

#134 Examining When One Is Most Engaged

Have students write for eight to 10 minutes in class on a time in their life when they felt most engaged. In their writing have them state why they thought this engagement occurred. Is it desirable to create this sense of engagement? Is it possible?

Following the writing, have students talk about their writing and the time of engagement. As the student describes this time and the assumptions implicit, other students should feed back the assumptions to the writers.

Process insights in the large group.

#135 *Building Stories, Assumptions*

Using the morning newspaper with its factual stories, have students work in groups of three and pick two or three stories in each group. Have them identify, or create, hidden assumptions beneath the stories to explain the stories.

#136 *Exploring an Assumption*

Have students write a simple declarative sentence that makes a statement of belief. This should illustrate a central assumption in the students' thinking. Here is an example of one such statement:

"People can achieve anything they can imagine if they try."

After making the initial statement, have students respond in writing to each of these four statements. Give students two to three minutes to respond to each question:

- ◆ Origin

  What experience(s) generated this belief or assumption? What causes the student to make the statement?

- ◆ Evidence

  Why is the statement true? What behavior supports it?

- ◆ Consequences

  What are the results stemming from this assumption? What related beliefs are implied?

- ◆ Alternative perspectives

  What other points of view exist that conflict with the stated assumption?

Following the completion of this writing assignment, put students in groups of three or four to discuss the writings.

After each group discusses their writings for 10 to 15 minutes, process answers in the large group.

#137 *Processing Perception*

Show students a 10-minute videotape of humans interacting. Try to select an excerpt lacking clarity of motive or intent.

Give students five minutes to write a summary of what they have just seen.

Put the students in small groups of three or four students to discuss how their perceptions differ, as well as their accounts. Process these in the large group.

#138 *Positing Assumptions*

Bring a photograph with multiple people in it. Ask students to interpret the photo. What has happened? What is happening? What are people thinking?

Process the comments in the large group.

#139 *Multicultural Perspective*

Have students write a three- to four-page paper describing "how a person from a culture other than yours would see you." In the paper have students detail characteristics of their own culture in some depth, while varying the interpretations.

In class create small-group discussion groups of two or three to share the perspectives in the writing.

#140 *Amplifying Multiple Choice*

As part of a multiple-choice test, select items in which the right answer requires reasoning. After the students indicate the response of their choice, they must write the reason for their response. Right answers require right reasoning.

#141 *Summarizing*

At a point before the midterm, have each student write a four- to five-page summary of the three or four key concepts of the course at that point. The paper should be informal, perhaps addressed to an imaginary classmate who missed most of the sessions. This will give the paper a tone conducive to understanding.

Have students share the papers in groups of two or three and then collect the papers.

#142 Using Questions on the Reading
Before giving a reading assignment, give students a set of specific textually oriented questions. These questions, linked to particular parts of the reading, create the structure for critical reading.

Have students write one- or two-sentence answers to each question. Then have them share their answers in small groups. If any questions remain after the small groups, treat them in front of the whole class.

#143 Identifying Thinking Misconceptions
Before the start of a course, identify the key misconceptions that students bring with them about the course. If possible, share this list with other faculty in the department.

At the start of the course, ask students if they can identify thought patterns that might hinder success in the course.

Have the students share their lists with each other in small groups and with the class. Give them your observations as well.

#144 Thinking Standards
After students have written an initial draft of a paper, list a set of standards that contrast effective, critical thinking from its opposite. Table 5.1 (above, right) includes examples of critical thinking standards.

Put students into groups of three to assess each other's papers in terms of these standards. To illustrate a good paper, hand out a model and comment on how it meets the standards.

Students should bring three copies of their

Table 5.1 Characteristics of Critical and Noncritical Thinking

Critical Thinking	Noncritical Thinking
Depth	Superficiality
Breadth	Narrowness
Significance	Triviality
Accuracy	Inaccuracy
Clarity	Lacking in clarity
Fairness	Prejudice

draft so each person can work simultaneously on reading and commenting. Have students take five minutes to make comments on the first page and sign off on that page when they have completed their comments. If students want an additional opinion, they can ask the faculty member.

#145 Comprehension/Noncomprehension
Ask students to take a minimum of two pages of notes on an assigned reading. One page should include notes on what the student understands and should include page references. The other page should focus on what the student does not understand and should include questions and page references.

This provides a much more disciplined basis for discussion in class. A fruitful way to proceed is to have small-group discussions of three or four students share what they do not understand.

Each group can then generate one question for the entire class that the group does not understand.

#146 Critical Reading and Problem Solving
In any problem-centered reading performed by stu-

dents, it is important for them to have a method of analysis. Here is one possible schemata for use:

◆ Definition and assumptions

What are the central terms? Are they clearly defined?

What are the core assumptions underlying the point of view of the writer?

◆ Conclusion and evidence

What conclusions are drawn? Why are they drawn? Are the conclusions supported by adequate evidence?

Is the evidence fair-minded? What is the source of the evidence? Are generalizations appropriately qualified?

◆ Reasoning about cause and effect

Is causality too simple in this model? Or is it appropriate in its complexity?

Is there logical consistency in the reasoning about cause and effect?

◆ Point of view

In stating a point of view, does the author distinguish factual statements from evaluative ones?

Are the value statements defensible?

Have students take notes using these categories and share their thoughts with other students in small groups; then process with the whole class.

This method works well on case studies.

#147 *Bottleneck Identification*
Near the end of the course, ask students to identify the point of most difficulty in the course. See if there is agreement among students on this point or points.

Ask what can be done to create more clarity in the course's development.

#148 *Clear Writing for Posterity*
In an attempt to focus students on clarity, give them a writing assignment to communicate with a future generation. Have them write an imaginary great-grandchild to help define the assignment.

Have students describe some aspect of contemporary life in detail. They should write as though the reader will know only through the writing.

With this specific audience and task in mind, students often write with more precision. With the freedom to select a topic, students choose the predictable and the unpredictable.

Classroom Assessment: Thinking about Thinking, Teaching, and Learning

To deepen the learning and teaching in any course, it is important to assess the quality of the classroom experience. Faculty need to know what students are learning in their classrooms as a result of their efforts. To do this, faculty need to engage in small-scale assessments during the academic term to ascertain student responses to the course. How well are students learning, and how well are faculty teaching?

The purpose of this classroom assessment is to improve teaching and learning in three ways:

♦ Focus students on their own learning of the knowledge and skills of the course and on how well their learning is proceeding. This purpose assumes an opportunity to improve learning through heightened motivation.

♦ Focus learners on their own values and attitudes as learners and on how they are responding to the teacher and teaching. This purpose involves metacognition about the quality of the students' own thinking. The goals of knowledge acquisition and intellectual skills development for the course can both be assessed.

♦ Focus the teacher on the teaching and on how well this is proceeding. This purpose assumes an opportunity to revise the methods of teaching.

By keeping these three purposes in mind, assessment assists both the student and the faculty member.

Students ask themselves, in a form of self-assessment, How am I performing in thinking and learning this course's skills and content? In reflecting, students turn the responsibility for their thinking and learning on themselves. It is hoped they recognize their own strengths and weaknesses as learners and thinkers in the specific context of that particular course and academic subject matter.

The second type of classroom assessment addresses the student's need for self-awareness about how one learns. It can range from thinking about how one thinks to how one responds to different pedagogical approaches by the faculty. This self-assessment is important in developing lifelong learning in students.

For the faculty member, gaining written assessment from students on the students' learning helps reveal what works and what doesn't. The knowledge thus gained allows for improvement. By focusing on what is not working, the faculty member can design the teaching process in alternative ways, implement that design, and learn how students respond through more student feedback. This process challenges the faculty member to improve continually. This process also helps faculty to identify the points in their courses where students get stuck.

In implementing these three types of classroom assessment, it is important to recognize the assumptions on which these goals are built. Two core sets of assumptions inform classroom assessment. The first recognizes that both teaching and learning can be improved. Corollaries of this assumption are that improved teaching leads to improved learning, and that feedback assists students and faculty in achieving their academic goals. Faculty need to clarify the goals of the course. A powerful faculty goal clarification tool is the "Teaching Goals Inventory" of Thomas A. Angelo and K. Patricia Cross, found in their *Classroom Assessment Techniques* (1993). In the inventory they identify six goal "clusters": higher-order thinking skills, basic academic success skills, discipline-specific knowledge and skills, liberal arts and academic values, work and career preparation, and personal development. Use of this tool, or other methods to clarify faculty goals, helps the improvement process.

A second core set of assumptions underlying the purposes of classroom assessment recognizes the centrality of the faculty and students in improving teaching and learning through assessment. It assumes that faculty and students can collaborate and motivate each other to enhance learning, and that faculty are best suited to structure and utilize the feedback from classroom assessment.

Assessing student learning is a complex process that is integral to college education. To assess in a way that measures student thinking, as well as the acquisition of information, faculty need to examine a variety of student behaviors. Classroom assessment involves a design phase, the assessment activity itself, and the follow-up to the assessment. Faculty need to examine the complex evolution of critical thinking by giving students multiple opportunities to demonstrate their abilities. Writing and speaking in all their various manifestations provide those opportunities. Before assessing the students, faculty should share their criteria. Following the learning activity, faculty assessment should include structured feedback linked to these criteria.

In classroom assessment, the goal is to improve teaching and learning. By overtly examining the teaching–learning process throughout the course and by providing continual feedback, the student and the faculty member both benefit.

THINKING ABOUT THINKING, TEACHING, AND LEARNING: CLASSROOM ASSESSMENT

#149 Self-Assessment: Focusing on an Earlier Piece of One's Analytic Writing
Have students look at an earlier piece of their own writing and scrutinize that piece of writing by answering a variety of questions:

- How much analysis and hypothesis occurs in the writing? How many patterns did you discern? Did these patterns surprise you?

- How much is the analysis linked to other texts, sources, and evidence? Are precise examinations of words treated?

- Did you look at multiple options in your analysis? Did you ask questions that made you think and ponder about the answer?

- Is there a link between the writing in the assignment and what's important in life? Why or why not?

- Where did the central idea in your paper come from? Did it change and evolve as you wrote?

- How complicated is the central question in your paper? Why is this question answered as you choose?

- Are there sections in your paper that could be improved? Where are they? How could they be improved?

#150 The One-Minute Paper (Angelo and Cross 1993)

Please answer each of the following questions in one or two sentences:

1. What was the most useful/meaningful thing you learned during this session?

2. What question(s) remain uppermost in your mind as we end this session?

#151 Directed Paraphrasing (Angelo and Cross 1993)

In no more than three concise sentences, summarize what you've learned about _____ in order to transmit that learning to an interested but skeptical colleague.

#152 The Muddiest Point (Angelo and Cross 1993)

What was the "muddiest" point in today's class? (In other words, what was least clear to you?)

#153 The RSQC2 Technique (Angelo and Cross 1993)

- Recall
  List the most interesting, significant, or useful points of the previous session.

- Summarize
  Summarize important points in one meaningful sentence.

- Question
  Raise any questions you have about that session.

- Comment
  Write down a word or phrase describing how you felt about that session while you were in it.

- Connect
  Connect what you learned in that session with what came before or comes next.

#154 Classroom Assessment: Reflection for Faculty and Students

At the end of each class, ask students to write for three to four minutes on some aspect of the preceding class. This feedback can be focused on the most delightful event of the class (or most alienating, bewildering, engaging, etc.). These short writings should be anonymous and focus on the affective domain of students' response.

#155 Assessing Collaboration

Before using small-group collaboration in class, have students write for five minutes on the characteristics of the best discussion they have experienced. In this list of characteristics, ask students to suggest any structural guidelines that would promote these positive characteristics.

After students complete the five-minute writing exercise, have students discuss their lists. Process these with the whole class to set expectations for collaboration in small groups.

#156 Assessing Time on Task and Study Method
In preparation for a test, ask students to keep track of how much time they spend studying for the test. In addition, ask them to detail how they studied. Collect this information before the test.

Share the results with the class to give them study ideas, as well as an indication of time on task.

Immediately before the test, ask students to predict their scores. Do this also immediately following taking the test.

In conjunction with sharing the earlier preparation data, ask students how they could have prepared better. Process this in the large group.

#157 Assessing for Problems
Before the middle of the course, ask students to assess any problems they are having. Structure a short five- to seven-minute writing exercise in which students address these questions in class:

◆ What is creating problems for you at this time?

◆ Is the source of the problem in the material, in the manner of teaching, or in your learning effort?

◆ What would help solve the problem? What can you do as a student? What can I do as the teacher?

Share the results, as appropriate, with the whole class.

#158 Self-Assessment and Ethnicity
In any course that attempts to study ethnicity and multiculturalism, incorporate this activity to personalize the issue of identity and ethnicity. Have students write for six to eight minutes in class on one of these questions:

◆ What feature of your own identity comes from your own ethnic, racial, or national background?

◆ When did you first meet someone dramatically different from yourself in terms of background? Did it create conflict or threaten your identity?

◆ Have you been belittled or humiliated because of your ethnic, racial, or national background? How did you feel then? Now? What was the source of the person's belittling behavior?

After they have written their responses, have students share these in small groups. Mix the groups so students talk with someone new. Process a few responses in the large group.

#159 Self-Assessment and Faculty Appointments
Mandate one or two office visits over a term per student, class size permitting. In the office visit, discuss the student's work by examining the student's portfolio. Students should keep all their writing, including in-class, short writings, in the portfolio.

After reviewing the student's writing and other pertinent matters, ask students to write 150 to 200 words of self-assessment on how they intend to evolve for the duration of the term.

#160 Thinking about Thinking
In any class ask students to think about their thinking in that course. This could be done early in the second half of the course. Students should answer these questions in an eight- to 10-minute writing exercise in class:

◆ What do you like best about your thinking in this class? What are your strengths?

◆ What do you like least about your thinking in this class? What are your weaknesses?

◆ How could you overcome your weaknesses?

◆ What has been the best of your thinking in this course?

Collect these short writings and respond with written comments.

#161 *Self-Grading and Team Paper Evaluation*

In any course in which a group paper/project is part of the grade, provide a vehicle for detailed input from each student. A form with the following questions can be used:

1. What was your role in the creation of the team paper?

2. How were the tasks divided among the group members?

3. What advantages did you find in working in a group?

4. What disadvantages?

5. What did you learn about working in teams from this assignment?

6. What did you learn about your topic that surprised you?

7. If you could do another paper with the same group, would you?

8. What would you change about the assignment or the group if you could?

9. How would you rate your performance in the team? What grade would you give yourself?

10. Please rate, by grade, the performance of others in your team. (This information will remain confidential.)

11. Overall, how would you rate the assignment? Comment here.

#162 *Portfolio Usage*

To assess the work of students for the grade in a course, have the students keep a portfolio of their work. Clarify two points at the start of the course.

First, state that you will randomly select from the writing. They will write a great deal, but you will not read all of it. An analogy to a sport's coach may help; a coach assigns many activities in practice but only assesses a portion. Second, state your desire for meaningful self-assessment and peer assessment for learning.

Papers also can be weighted, with less emphasis on randomly graded work in the first third of the course and more emphasis in the last third.

While a variety of writing should go into the portfolio, the focal point of the writing should be to demonstrate the thinking and reasoned judgment of the student.

#163 *Grading and Assessment*

For short writing assignments that you wish to grade, do so with a simple grading system. Use a three-point scale of full/half/none on these shorter assignments. Distribute an example of a full-credit piece of writing.

#164 *Study: Self-Assessment*

At the first class session following the midterm, ask students to write their responses on their study habits:

◆ How did you study?

◆ How long did you study?

◆ How much time did you devote to reading?

◆ How do you read?

Link the test to their studying habits:

◆ Which test questions made you work the hardest? Why?

◆ Could you study in a way to alleviate this difficulty?

If class time is short, students could do this exercise on their own time, outside class. With more time, students could discuss their responses in small groups, process them with the whole class, and hand them in.

#165 What's Left to Learn

At a point in the second half of the course, ask students to write down the three main points they've learned so far.

Ask them what they believe they have left to learn in the course.

If time permits, these exercises can be expanded to include asking what they have learned so far in their undergraduate education and what they have left to learn in their undergraduate education.

#166 Faculty Self-Assessment

In course syllabi, faculty state the course objectives that they have selected for students. Read your syllabus for a given course. Ask yourself two kinds of questions:

- How do I teach these objectives to students? At what points in the course are they taught?

- How do I assess the student achievement of these objectives? How do the students know how they're doing?

Adjust your teaching accordingly.

#167 Remember and Link

At the start of each class, many faculty recall and summarize the key points from the previous class in lecture format.

As an alternative plan, ask students to remember five key points from the last class. This can be done by recalling short phrases or key terms. Have them rank the five points in order of importance. Then ask for the first and second items from the class to put on the board. You are ready for commentary to link these points to the direction of the upcoming class.

#168 Feedback on Learning

After approximately one-third of the course has been completed, ask the class for anonymous input on four specific questions.

- What is hindering learning in class?

- What specifically could the instructor and the class do to stop the hindering of learning?

- What is aiding students in learning?

- What concrete steps could the instructor and the class take to improve learning?

Collect these and respond by changing, if appropriate. Let students know the results of the feedback.

#169 Pause in the Lecture

At a point in the beginning of a lecture, tell students that you have set a timer for approximately the middle of the lecture. You will ask them to pause for a short writing assignment when the buzzer sounds.

When the buzzer goes off, ask the students to write on how engaged and attentive they were to the course material and dynamics immediately before pausing. How has their attention level assisted or hindered their learning?

Collect short, 100-word responses.

#170 History: One-Minute Response

In a modern world history course, ask students to spend one minute writing on two questions:

- Why did England rule the world stage in the 19th century?

- What is one question that you have at this point about the course material?

This activity can be repeated to gain more detail on student thinking about the course dynamics by focusing the questions more specifically.

#171 *Anthropological Observation*

In an introductory anthropology class, ask students to watch closely a videotape on a particular culture. Then, after the viewing concludes, ask them to write a list of phrases summarizing the culture.

Process the list and put the items on the board. The list will show students they can, through observation, make meaningful judgments and assessments about culture. The list also provides an opportunity for you to clarify and deepen their understanding.

#172 *Study: Self-Assessment*

Ask students to keep track of their study habits over a week. This self-assessment should include information on these items:

◆ When did you study?

◆ How long did you study?

◆ Where did you study?

◆ How productive was your studying in terms of learning?

After making these observations, ask the students if any patterns emerged that could improve their learning.

Conclusion

For many years colleges and universities have refined their teaching mission using references to "providing instruction." When the majority of higher education faculty examined their role in teaching and providing instruction, they identified their role in this mission as the delivery personnel who instructed through lectures.

Although there are notable exceptions at all colleges and universities, most faculty delivering instruction adhered to the following model:

- Faculty transferred their knowledge to the student. Faculty expertise in the subject matter was the most important variable. The core faculty responsibility was to cover the material. The better the lecture coverage of the material, the greater the faculty success in providing instruction, or "good teaching." Teachers were experts. The input of the expertise through the lecture was teaching.

- Students were viewed as empty vessels to be filled with "deposits" of faculty knowledge. Students were passive recipients who memorized the information directed at them. They existed in relative isolation in a college classroom.

- The dynamics in this model are between a powerful, authoritative faculty and a quiet, relatively submissive group of students. Students competed with each other in an individualistic context. Often, students were assessed on the basis of true–false or multiple-choice questions. An environment of objective anonymity characterized the personal dynamics among students and between faculty and students.

Until relatively recently, this instructional model seemed to be achieving its goals. Students succeeded or failed in this academic world. Most people believed that failure showed a lack of effort on the students' part, not on the part of the faculty member or on the part of the model of instructional delivery itself.

PROBLEMS WITH FACULTY INSTRUCTIONAL DELIVERY

In the past decade, research has demonstrated that lecture teaching is not the best way to facilitate student learning, particularly in the areas of critical thinking and critical literacy. While teachers lecture, students are focused on the lecture for two-thirds of the time at best, according to the research. As a lecture goes on, student attentiveness weakens. Retention of material in the last 10 minutes of a lecture is less than one-third of what it is in the first 10 minutes (Meyers and Jones 1993). Over time, lecture-based learning fades.

In addition to research documenting the shortcomings of the lecture method, cognitive research also demonstrated that people learn in a variety of different ways. An undue reliance on one method of teaching, such as the lecture, deprives students of using other ways to learn.

Criticism from society added to that from educational researchers. Employers reported that graduates and former students of higher education often had memorized facts but could not demonstrate higher-order thinking skills. They complained of the inability of employees to solve problems through analysis and conclusions.

Regardless of the source of the criticism and problem identification, the detachment, disengagement, and passivity of students and former students came to be seen as highly undesirable.

ACTIVE STUDENT LEARNING: EVOLUTION OF A NEW MODEL

Growing numbers of faculty sensed that the instructional delivery, lecture model was not working. Student disinterest and criticism grew. Many faculty searched for a more vital way to teach. They began to look for new ways to engage their students. Faculty came to believe that students needed to be actors in their own development.

Since the early 1980s, four movements have grown among higher education faculty to improve teaching and learning:

- critical thinking
- writing across the curriculum
- collaborative, team learning
- classroom assessment

All four of these movements place emphasis on student learning as the end and faculty teaching as the means to that end. All four of these movements emphasize the need for an active orientation by students.

The central strategies by which faculty develop learning and improved thinking in students require student engagement in activity. Primarily, faculty do this by structuring student writing and speaking in conjunction with reading and listening; in these ways students make their thinking known. In *Promoting Active Learning*, Meyers and Jones offer this analysis of active learning:

"Active learning derives from two basic assumptions: (1) that learning is by nature an active endeavor and (2) that different people learn in different ways. Two teaching corollaries seem to follow from these assumptions: first, that students learn best when applying subject matter—in other words, learning by doing; second, that teachers who rely exclusively on any one teaching approach often fail to get through to significant numbers of students" (1993, xi).

Helping students become active learners (critical readers, critical listeners, critical writers, and critical speakers) required more depth and less breadth in the curriculum. Learning that persists stems from in-depth experiences; broadly-based learning of facts is soon forgotten. Inquiry and questioning are central to active learning.

Students, through activities, must distinguish what they know from what they don't know. This involves an intellectual search for knowledge, as well as for values. In this process students need to create their own synthesis of knowledge while reflecting the standards of the intellectual life. These standards include precision, coherence, sufficiency, breadth, and accuracy. Students learn how to think well, not what to think.

In addition to drawing on faculty expertise, students need to draw on the knowledge base of other students. Much student experience is rooted in misinformation, misconception, ignorance, bias, and prejudice. Active learning strategies, informed by critical thinking, are required for transformation of both students and faculty.

Faculty and students focused on improving teaching and learning through new approaches are developing a new model. That model, active student learning, contains the following characteristics:

- Faculty facilitate student learning through the creation of opportunities for students to think. Faculty become more focused on pedagogy and how to promote student learning. Their core activity becomes designing active learning strategies for students to learn. Faculty become concerned with student ability to manifest their learning in specific ways.

- Students, in the active learning model, are engaged in creating their own knowledge. Through thinking, they develop their own competencies and capabilities. Students discover the world of ideas. They learn to solve problems, generate ideas, form and apply concepts, design systematic plans of action, explore issues from multiple perspectives, carefully analyze situations, discuss subjects in an organized way, and use language critically. Students often engage actively in these learning behaviors with other students.

- The dynamics in the student active learning model involve faculty willingly sharing time and decision making with students. Cooperation and collaboration among students, and between students and faculty, become hallmark traits. Students constantly give feedback on the progress of their learning while faculty solicit suggestions on how to facilitate learning better. Faculty and students are actively engaged in learning.

DILEMMA: HOW TO PROMOTE THE MODEL OF ACTIVE STUDENT LEARNING

Faculty need to design learning strategies in which students engage in tasks to promote their intellectual skills development. For students to improve their critical judgment, they need practice at thinking, both on their own and in groups. Faculty need to create exercises and assignments through which students receive coaching and constructive feedback about their thinking. This is not to imply that lecturing is outmoded. Good lectures have had, and will continue to have, great value. Rather, it is important to see the lecture as a method, not the method, among a repertoire of pedagogies. Among many faculty relying exclusively on the lecture, there is a disturbing sense that something is not working. This sense is testimony to the need for additional strategies. In the process of creating active learning strategies, faculty should draw on the diverse background of their students in the activities. By developing a repertoire of active learning strategies, faculty will be better able to find a fit with the diverse learning styles of their students.

A deficiency of knowledge exists relative to the practice and application of active learning strategies. At present, there is no resource of active learning strategies within the various academic disciplines. Anecdotes and piecemeal approaches abound, but there is no systematic effort to provide teaching faculty with a menu of disciplinary strategies on how to teach thinking in the disciplines. Some faculty have shared their innovations with colleagues, but these efforts have been sporadic and limited to the most creative teachers.

SOLUTION: FACULTY SHARE BEST PRACTICES IN IMPLEMENTING ACTIVE STUDENT LEARNING

The way to build a new tradition of teaching and learning is through faculty sharing with each other what works and what does not. This focus on creating a culture of "best practices" in teaching and learning requires sustained time and energy to succeed. This book attempts to assist in the successful creation of that sharing culture.

While successful faculty teaching obviously requires subject matter knowledge and personal, committed authenticity, faculty cannot improve without some idea of how to improve. Most schemes that identify a process for the evolution of a faculty member's teaching begin with the idea of gathering information. Information gathering occurs around two areas. First, the faculty member reflects on his or her own behavior, how it affects students, and what assumptions underlie one's own behavior. Second, the faculty member gathers information on the options available in terms of instructional strategies, techniques, and practices, as well as on the assumptions underlying the options.

This book focuses on this second aspect. It is hoped that faculty will disseminate these active learning approaches to build learning communities among each other and improve teaching. Through the use, evaluation, and revision of active learning approaches, faculty can help students think in a more thorough fashion about their lives and values, and can assess student learning more precisely to determine student competence. Through active learning, students will achieve a better sense of themselves as learners and thinkers.

Bibliography

Adler, Mortimer J. 1982. *The Paideia Proposal.* New York: Simon and Schuster.

Angelo, Thomas A., and K. Patricia Cross. 1993. *Classroom Assessment Techniques.* San Francisco: Jossey-Bass.

Barnes, Cynthia A., ed. 1992. *Critical Thinking: Educational Imperative.* New Directions for Community Colleges. San Francisco: Jossey-Bass.

Bloom, Benjamin S. 1956. *Taxonomy of Educational Objectives.* New York: David McKay.

Bouton, Clark, and Russell Y. Garth, eds. 1983. *Learning in Groups.* San Francisco: Jossey-Bass.

Boyer, Ernest L. 1990. *Scholarship Reconsidered.* Princeton, N.J.: Carnegie Foundation for the Advancement of Teaching.

Brookfield, Stephen D. 1995. *Becoming a Critically Reflective Teacher.* San Francisco: Jossey-Bass.

———. 1991. *Developing Critical Thinkers.* San Francisco: Jossey-Bass.

———. 1990. *The Skillful Teacher.* San Francisco: Jossey-Bass.

Chaffee, John. 1991. *Thinking Critically.* Boston: Houghton Mifflin.

Chickering, Arthur W., and Zelda F. Gamson. 1990. "Seven Principles for Good Practice in Undergraduate Education." *The Wingspread Journal* , 1–3.

Chickering, Arthur W., and Zelda F. Gamson, eds. 1991. *Applying the Seven Principles for Good Practice in Undergraduate Education.* San Francisco: Jossey-Bass.

Eble, Kenneth E. 1988. *The Craft of Teaching.* San Francisco: Jossey-Bass.

Ennis, Robert. 1962. "A Concept of Critical Thinking." *Harvard Educational Review* 32: 81–111.

Gabelnick, Faith, et al. 1990. *Learning Communities: Creating Connections Among Students, Faculty, and Disciplines.* San Francisco: Jossey-Bass.

Goodsell, Anne, et al. 1992. *Collaborative Learning: A Sourcebook for Higher Education.* University Park, Pa.: Pennsylvania State University, National Center on Postsecondary Teaching, Learning, and Assessment.

Involvement in Learning: Realizing the Potential of America's Higher Education. 1984. Final report of the Study Group on the Conditions of Excellence in American Higher Education, sponsored by the National Institute of Education, U.S. Department of Education. Washington, D.C.: U.S. Government Printing Office.

Kuhn, Thomas S. 1970. *The Structure of Scientific Revolutions.* 2d ed. Chicago: University of Chicago Press.

McPeck, John. 1981. *Critical Thinking and Education.* New York: St. Martin's Press.

Meadows, Donella H. 1972. *The Limits to Growth.* New York: Universe Books.

Meyers, Chet. 1991. *Teaching Students to Think Critically.* San Francisco: Jossey-Bass.

Meyers, Chet, and Thomas B. Jones. 1993. *Promoting Active Learning.* San Francisco: Jossey-Bass.

National Profile of Community Colleges: Trends and Statistics 1997–1998. 1997. Washington, D.C.: Community College Press, American Association of Community Colleges.

O'Banion, Terry, and Associates. 1994. *Teaching and Learning in the Community College.* Washington, D.C.: Community College Press, American Association of Community Colleges.

Paul, Richard. 1990. *Critical Thinking.* Rohnert Park, Calif.: Center for Critical Thinking and Moral Critique, Sonoma State University.

Peterson, Joel. 1994. "Twenty-Three Skills and Dispositions of Effective Thinking Targeted for Curricular Emphasis in the Minnesota Community College System." *Third Annual and Summary Report to the Bush Foundation, 1991–1994.* St. Paul: Minnesota Community Colleges.

Roueche, John E., and George A. Baker III. 1987. *Access and Excellence.* Washington, D.C.: Community

College Press, American Association of Community Colleges.

Schwartz, Robert J., and David N. Perkins. 1990. *Teaching Thinking: Issues and Approaches.* Pacific Grove, Calif.: Midwest Publications.

U.S. Department of Labor. *What Work Requires of Schools: A SCANS Report for America 2000.* 1991. Assembled by the Secretary's Commission on Achieving Necessary Skills, U.S. Department of Labor. Washington, D.C.: U.S. Government Printing Office.

White, Edward M. 1994. *Teaching and Assessing Writing.* 2d ed. San Francisco: Jossey-Bass.

Wingspread Group on Higher Education. 1993. *An American Imperative: Higher Expectations for Higher Education.* Racine, Wis.: Johnson Foundation, Inc.

Index